OUR STORIES AND OUR SONGS

THE CELTIC SUPPORT

By Liam Kelly

For all Celtic fans, particularly those that have been so kind as to help me with travel and match tickets throughout the years. Special mentions to Pete, Brian and Gerry Duffy, the Port Glasgow Emerald CSC members, Michael Burt, John Cowan and John Davila.

Not forgetting my family trinity: Mum, Dad and Bethany.

Acknowledgements

Firstly, to all Celtic supporters worldwide, I thank you dearly. Your unequivocal backing is the greatest and ultimate inspiration behind the book. I am blessed to be among you.

The help that I have received from the Celtic family to make this publication possible has been quite unbelievable. As such, I have a number of people to be thankful to.

To those that supported my project with pictures, stories and contributions; I am forever indebted. The platform for requesting responses, from countless social media and forum sites has been incredible. Not least the administrators on the Green Brigade forum, who also allowed me to use multiple images. I only hope that my piece on the group does them justice.

Special thanks must go to Vagelis Georgariou for the fantastic photo that he allowed me to use for the front cover. Paul Cuddihy at 'Celtic View' also played a key role in getting hold of the photo and others.

Photo archivist, Brian Gallagher, very kindly donated me a selection of fantastic images from as early as the 1920s up until the present decade. His gesture is greatly appreciated and the book would certainly be a lesser production without them.

Also on the image front, Jamie Fox sent me some photographs from him fabulous collection, which stretches as far back as the 1890s. The photographs provide a great source of intrigue and are some of the rarest found of the Club.

I owe Martin Beatty a depth of gratitude for allowing me to donate proceeds from the book to the family charity: 'Down's & Proud'. Furthermore, his help in interviewing his son, Jay was of real benefit.

Jay and each of the people that I interviewed throughout the writing process have been an honour to speak to. I thoroughly enjoyed putting questions to former players, prominent fans and people from outside of the Club. The insight that I have received from them has been very humbling and interesting.

Thanks must go to Stephen Dennie for the article that he kindly donated to my history chapter, Omar Ibrahim for the editing in the early stages and to members of the Green Brigade forum site. Without their input, the publication would be a shadow of itself and frankly, a disorganised mess. Unreserved thanks also go to David Tracey for his assistance in this regard.

The generous help of Fred McNeill to suggest a range of ideas and a foreword is much appreciated and that appreciation extends to both Matt McGlone and Paul Brennan for agreeing to pen the pieces.

When I needed imagery, information and promotion of the book, tremendous help was at hand courtesy of Stephen Murray and Andrew Reilly. I cannot express my thanks enough to the pair of you.

I thank my uncle, Des Kelly, for his continued editing, advice and support. He has worked tirelessly with me.

Last and by no means least, the encyclopaedic site that is 'The Celtic Wiki' has been of tremendous help with a wide range of dates, figures and information. It has been my go to site for confirmation on different moments in our superb history.

Contents

Foreword by Matt McGlone

Whenever I'm writing about Celtic and the Club's supporters, the first word that comes into my head is 'identity'. When writing the foreword for this book and what you're about to read throughout its pages, that identity and unbreakable bond between the Club and the support shows why it's so very special.

Being a Celtic fan isn't just about going to the games on a Saturday or whenever. It isn't just about the want to win trophies on the field of play, always striving to be the winner. And it isn't about shouting 'we're the best'. No it's all about who we are as people.

It's about the way you conduct yourself in life, your morals, your attitude and approach to matters of charity – along with the in-built want to try and help others less fortunate than yourself. All these factors create who you are. In fact, all the above attributes mentioned in being a Celtic fan, are the very reasons this very book was created. There is a spirit in this read, which combines winning and losing and laughing and crying. Being a Celtic fan is a journey. In fact, the late great Tommy Burns described it to me once as a 'rollercoaster' and how right he was. It can't all be about winning, being a Celtic fan carries its own badges of agony.

Celtic as we know was founded for charitable purposes but the Club, as it evolved through the decades, became more and more distant from its original roots. But it's made a recovery and those roots are growing now more than they've ever done. That recovery is all down to the supporters. The amount of supporter led initiatives and charitable groups that exist within the Celtic family today is truly astonishing. Whether it's rattling a can, to climbing a mountain and all else in between, the support are leading the way raising pennies and pounds for those who are ill, who are needy, who need to be kept alive on expensive drugs and so on.

Something that may well never have crossed your mind, is the charitable donations and the work carried out to raise those donations, are all carried out on the vast majority of occasions by fans in aid of people they have never met in their life. They are raising funds because it matters. They are raising funds because others need it.

When the call is made the support spring into action and I doubt very much if there are supporters in any other football club world-wide who are our charitable equal. Knowing the personality of the person or the group in need simply doesn't come into it. The author of this very book thought about writing it because he saw it as a vehicle to raise charitable funds. He's done that and the ball rolls on from here.

We have our legends, we have our heroes and we have some wonderful life moments supporting this great club of ours. When Brother Walfrid sailed across the Irish Sea he didn't just bring a vision and a dream that became a reality. No, he also gave us our identity which you'll carry throughout your life with you. It's very special, wrap your arms around it, look after it, pass it on to the next generation and be very proud of it, and never let it out of your sight!

Foreword by Paul Brennan

As Celtic supporters we sing 'if you know your history' but that history is now vast and is well into its second century, so actually knowing all of that history is near impossible. While the great triumphs on the field have been documented in great detail, the story of the Celtic supports has received little coverage by comparison. Since the decision was taken in 1887 in St Mary's Hall to form a football team, a community claimed Celtic as their own. It started in the impoverished streets of the east end of Glasgow, and soon found adherents wherever images of the green and white hoops went.

'Our Stories And Our Songs' recognises that the story of Celtic, the story of any football club, is more than results and trophies, more than great players and on-field drama, it's the story of those people who raised their voices in triumph, or who carried the Club's traditions during the long, hard, winter years, when success seemed a forlorn hope.

A great strength of the support has been its communal voice. We are taken back to 'God Save Ireland', sung in unison by the Celtic and Hibernian supporters in 1911, a song which had resonance from the very early years of Celtic history, but it's not all heavy sentiment. Readers of a certain age will give a knowing smile when recalling 'Ten men won the league, tra-la-la-la-la'.

Winning titles and trophies is something we've been gotten used to in recent years but some will always stand out in the memory as special. Every Celtic fan who was alive in 1986 will remember the sheer joy when, against all odds,

Celtic won the league at Love St, as Hearts capitulated at Dens Park. The Centenary Season too is given its place as a remarkable era in Celtic history. Celtic were simply imperious that season as the fans took advantage of the times by singing 'Happy Birthday Dear Celtic'.

The 1990s is likely to be a short chapter in any Celtic book. The decade was synonymous with defeat on the park as the memory of our great 'Nine-in-a-row' boast was violated, but even through this era, the Celtic support found their voice and their purpose. The 'St Patrick's Day massacre' is relived, as well as that incredible night in 1996 at Celtic Park against Aberdeen. Celtic were not quite back on top but they were on their way, and when Jorge Cadete came off the bench to make his debut, then lifted the ball over the onrushing Aberdeen keeper to score, we knew we had a special player.

Celtic won nothing in season 2002-03 but no account of the Celtic support would be complete without mention of this very special time in our history. FIFA and UEFA don't often hand out their annual Fair Play awards to a group of fans, but that's what happened. Celtic rediscovered their European appetitive with wins over Liverpool, Celta Vigo and Stuttgart on the road to the UEFA Cup Final in Seville. The joy and entertainment from that season remains a highlight for many of us. Some enlightened individual realised it would be appropriate for us to share our Spanish joy at Ibrox by bringing beach balls. The sight of one end of the Ibrox pitch covered in beach balls a moment before the game was due to start encapsulates much of what you need to know about the Celtic support.

Then came Seville itself. 80,000 Celtic fans descended on the city, which soon ran out of pretty much everything. As the day progressed, food and beer were shipped in from beyond the Andalucía region to keep the bars and restaurants open. Beds had long been sequestered from the Spanish beach resorts as hotel room were given a temporary increase in capacity.

Lisbon is also given its appropriate place in the book. Thousands of Celtic fans left Britain for the first time. They turned up in the sweltering Lisbon heat in shirts and ties, but what they and the Lions did is still recalled across the continent.

The sheer size of the support overwhelmed in Lisbon and Seville but this is nothing new. The record attendance for a European Cup game and for a domestic game in Europe each involved Celtic. 'Our Stories And Our Songs' is an historical record of a people, their values, hopes and dreams.

Introduction

Celtic Football Club can boast a very literate heritage. The creation of 'Shamrock' fanzine and the official 'Celtic View' magazine, in the 1960s, were the first of their kind in British football. Countless documents, poems and books have been written both before and since, each adding to our unrivalled collection of writings.

The endless scripture surrounding the Club led me to increasingly enjoy writing and for some time I thought about where I'd like to go with that interest. Thinking on, I decided that I would aim to produce my own book. So it was, in January 2013, that I started to make my idea a reality and write about the supporters of Celtic. Given my unquenchable love for the Club and above all, the fans, I could not think of a greater angle from which to write.

Cooped up in the back of the family car, strangely on the evening that St Mirren had knocked Celtic out of the League Cup; I set the wheels in motion and began drawing up a contents page.

My family and I were returning from a visit to see my grandparents, who we had just dropped off for evening mass at their local Catholic Church. There was a tired silence that afforded me the opportunity to reflect on the conversation that Grandad and I had enjoyed that day.

Grandad had told me how he fled his native County Offaly in the fifties', like many of his Irish compatriots seeking work in the UK. He went on to explain that he found employment as a crane driver in a small village named Godstone in Surrey. There, he met and married my grandmother, later raising my dad and his two brothers on a local council estate.

I couldn't help but think how different my mother's upbringing must have been. Mum's parents ran a kitchen showroom and a successful newsagent on the south coast in Bournemouth. Her side of the family is also almost wholly English and has always been based on the southern shores of the country.

I live with my parents and younger sister in the beautiful seaside town of Poole in Dorset. The blend of my mother's angle and life in an elegant part of the world, with my father's Irish working class influences, certainly shapes my character and indeed my support of Celtic.

It has been my aim to learn from elements in both sides of the family throughout my life. I have done exactly that since working on this book and I am pleased to have undertaken further writing roles in the Celtic world. This has been achieved through a blog for 'TAL' fanzine and latterly with 'Celtic Quick News'.

The composition of 'Our Stories And Our Songs' has allowed me to meet some great people in places such as Port Glasgow, Falkirk, Belfast and Myrtle Beach! I have made new and unbreakable friendships and have enjoyed every moment that I've spent connecting with my journey.

In keeping with the traditions of the Club, I have decided to donate all proceeds from the book to 'Down's & Proud'. The charity was set up by Jay Beatty's mother, Áine, in 2007. It aims to benefit families affected by Down syndrome, through allowing them to share experiences and support one other.

'Down's & Proud' places its impetuous on the wonderful children, who have each touched their families in a special way. Hopefully the book will sell well enough to fund a day out for the children involved with the support group.

I hope that my project turns out to be an enjoyable and entertaining read.

Hail Hail!

Foundations & Roots

In a recent Champions League campaign, Celtic enjoyed one of the finest results of its illustrious history. Who could forget that famous night when the Hoops beat Barcelona 2-1? Andres Iniesta described the support that evening in the following way: "The Celtic fans are very special and the Club and players can be very proud of them. They are the best I have ever heard." There certainly is something extraordinary at Celtic, a sense of belonging to an institution far greater than a football club. Perhaps this can be linked to the Club's foundations and roots.

Celtic was of course primarily born amidst a time of suffering and was founded for charitable purposes. Though there is much more to the Celtic story and the mystique that surrounds it.

Undoubtedly, the Club would not have come into being had the famine in Ireland not taken place. The Irish famine between 1845 and 1852 was a period that caused widespread starvation, death and emigration. The Irish scattered themselves around the world, with a large number of these refugees fleeing to Glasgow. The majority of those men, women and children resided in a very run down area of the city's east end; north of the river Clyde - known as the Garngad. The Garngad was home to some of the great legends of the Celtic story, none more so than the Club's record goal scorer, James McGrory. Others of the immigrants settled in slums around the poorest districts of Glasgow; from the Gorbals to Govan and as far as Paisley. Living conditions were basic to say the least and the welcome that the Irish exiles received from the indigenous population was less than hospitable. There was little sympathy for their plight and often open racism. They were regarded as alien, largely due to nationality and Catholic faith. Indeed it could be suggested that the refugees found themselves in a similar struggle to that of their homeland.

Expatriates from across the sea again found themselves to be starving and unable to support their families. Some had to abandon their faith and convert to become Protestant, for it was only by that means that they would be welcomed into soup kitchens. Due to institutional discrimination, employment opportunities were very limited for the Irish in the west of Scotland too. The most common of very few occupations available: factory work in the surrounding area of the Garngad. Most men in this region sought employment at the factory and the women took care of domestic life. Other breadwinners tended to seek work in the shipbuilding, coal mining and service industries.

Fortunately, Irish Marist Brother, Andrew Kerins, who was better known by his adopted clerical name, Brother Walfrid; would have a vision that changed social conditions dramatically. Walfrid was sent to teach in St Mary's School on Abercromby Street in Glasgow during the mid-1800s. The school was headed by another Marist Brother named Dorotheus. Brother Dorotheus had much admiration for the work of his confrere and was quick in spotting Walfrid's talents. He supported and encouraged the Irishman's various charitable projects.

In 1874, Walfrid was given his own new school to manage (Sacred Heart in Bridgeton). He had set up a charity called 'The Poor Children's Dinner Table' a decade later, with the sole aim of providing meals for the children of Glasgow's east end. Dorotheus assisted Walfrid with the operation of the charity and together, they were soon providing over a thousand meals per week for the child occupants of the Calton area.

However, the idea of forming Celtic Football Club was engendered through Walfrid's invitational visit to a reception for Hibernian FC. Hibernian, the Roman name for Ireland, had been formed in Edinburgh, by Catholic priests twelve years earlier. In those twelve years, they had managed to win the Scottish Cup and it was for that reason that they held the reception. During the celebrations, the Secretary of Hibernian challenged the Irish Catholic guests to assemble a football club of their own. The event then closed with a profound rendition of 'God Save Ireland', the unofficial national anthem for Home Rule advocates in that era!

Based on what he had just seen, Walfrid envisaged the creation of his own football club but sought to expand upon the 'Hibs' template. It soon became apparent that Brother Dorotheus shared his enthusiasm for such a phenomenon. Walfrid scheduled a meeting in St. Mary's Roman Catholic Church in the Calton on November 6th 1887. With the aid of his colleague (Brother Dorotheus), John Glass (whom a certain Willie Maley claimed: "Celtic owes their very existence") ; Hugh Darroch, Michael Cairns, Dr John Conway, John H McLaughlin, Joseph Nelis and Joseph Shaughnessy – a post meeting announcement was proclaimed. "A football team will be formed for the maintenance of dinner tables for the children and the unemployed." The Club prioritised that raison d'être within the parishes of St Mary's (Calton), Sacred Heart (Bridgeton) and St Michael's (Parkhead). These were areas where infant mortality and poverty were rife. The sect of the communities in need of most help was that consisting of the Irish. However, Celtic would be an inclusive Club, openly willing to help anybody that required its assistance.

The Club also had a smaller aim: bridging the gap between the native Glaswegians and the Irish influx. Walfrid and his team of assistants recognised the need for social integration. They wanted a football club that Scottish, Irish, Protestant and Catholic people alike could support. This is reflected in the selection of the Club's name: 'Celtic'. In days gone by, there had been numerous short lived clubs of the emerald emigrate in Scotland... not least 'Shamrocks' and 'Eirann Rangers'. Their identities were too exclusive. Their vision short sighted. Celtic did not make that error.

The widely mistaken thought amongst many Celtic fans is that the Club was named with a soft sounding 'C', the very way that it is pronounced today. However, the originally intended name was with a hard 'C' sounding as a 'K'. This name has its origins from the Ancient Celts and represented the Scottish and Irish cultural blend. The adoption of the present pronunciation was somewhat less romantic than a clever invention by Walfrid et al. It was in fact likely adopted due to the accents of the Club's supporters!

As of December 1887, Celtic had themselves a manager and first player, in essence. A man named Pat Welsh was paramount to this double acquisition. Welsh was a Fenian activist, who twenty years earlier had attempted to evade crown forces by escaping through Dublin docks. At the river Liffey he was spotted by a certain Sergeant Maley; an Irishman wrestling with his conscience whilst serving in the British Army. Welsh gave Mr. Maley his word that he would refrain from his revolutionary actions if he were allowed to board the boat to Scotland. His wish was granted.

Pat Welsh settled in Glasgow, where he became renowned as a master tailor, working on Buchanan Street. He also gained respect in St Mary's parish. Pat remembered Sergeant Maley's gesture and when the father of Willie and Tom retired, he invited him to move to Glasgow. The invitation was accepted.

Welsh eventually took Brother Walfrid and John Glass to the Maley household in Cathcart. They visited with a proposition to the eldest son Tom, a revered player at Hibernian, to join in the new Celtic Football Club. The legend goes that Tom was not at home so the Celtic delegation started chatting to his brother, Willie. They had asked for Tom to contact them with a response. Whilst leaving, Brother Walfrid turned back to the house and said to Willie: "Why don't you come as well?" After his initial modesty was shunned, Willie was persuaded to sign for Celtic. When Tom heard about the visit, he communicated with the Celtic founders immediately and agreed to join his brother at the Club. The visit led to a reciprocal love affair between the Maley's and Celtic, which lasted for over half a century!

In 1888 the founders of Celtic Football Club pleaded for donations, in order to commence work on a stadium, acquire players and secure match fixtures. There are forty five acknowledged donators and their contributions were sufficient to get the Club underway. At this point in the Celtic timeline, the position of John Glass was of great import. Glass, a joiner by trade, proved astute in enlisting the help of many useful contacts within the building industry. Furthermore, he was a larger than life character, with a strong personality. Through his networking, he managed to attract many reputable footballers to the Club. In turn, the names attracted large crowds with well-behaved disposition.

A ground was secured on Dalmarnock Road. The Club took it on lease for five years at a rental fee of £50 annually. Two stands were to be built and a cinder track, twelve feet broad, circulating the field. The stands were erected and playing surface prepared, by a large band of volunteers. The volunteers worked long hours, without pay for their tireless labour. Materials, plans and guidance were offered courtesy of John Glass and his array of experienced contacts. Inside six months the stands had been constructed. The stadium was readily prepared for its first match and the legend that is Celtic Football Club began.

On the 28th May 1888, Celtic played host to a (Oldco) Rangers eleven in a friendly match. This was the first official game at Celtic Park. The fixture drew a crowd of two thousand. 'The Bhoys' team was comprised of guest players, who took to the field with quite different attire from the traditional hoops seen today. Instead, they sported white shirts with a dark collar, bearing a red Celtic cross upon the breast; black shorts and emerald green socks. The line-up was as follows:

Michael Dolan – Goalkeeper
Eddie Pearson – Right back
James McLaughlin – Left back
Willie Maley – Right half back
James Kelly (C) – Centre half back
Phil Murray – Left half back
Neil McCallum- Outside right
Tom Maley- Inside right
John Madden- Centre
Michael Dunbar- Inside left
Charlie Gorevin- Outside left

McCallum netted to give Celtic the lead, gaining the accolade of the Club's first ever goal scorer. Added to the score sheet were Kelly and Tom Maley. Maley scored a hat-trick! In reply, (Oldco) Rangers' Soutar bagged a brace. The final score was Celtic 5-2 (Oldco) Rangers.

As a result of the game, the two clubs formed a close relationship! Players from both sides trained together and shared travel when visiting away grounds for friendly fixtures outside of Glasgow and for ventures down South in particular.

By September, Celtic had entered their first competitive tournament – the Scottish Cup. The Club reached the final, held at Hampden Park in 1889. Opposition then was in the form of now deceased, Third Lanark. Playing in front of a crowd of eighteen thousand, Third Lanark eased to victory by three goals to nil. However, the game was ordered to be re-played as a result of heavy snowfall. In the replay, Third Lanark again took victory, this time by a solitary goal, winning 2-1. Amidst such valiant achievement, the principle of charity was not lost. The Club donated a sum of £421 to Catholic charities at the end of that season; this all the more commendable when you consider that the only competitive football was offered in the Scottish Cup.

In the year of 1890, a committee was established with each of the founders having an assigned role ranging from mere membership to some of the more formal responsibilities.

As Celtic Football Club grew in stature, attendances grew with it. Based on the format of professional football in the English leagues, many Scottish clubs decided to follow suit. It was proposed that Celtic join the Scottish Football League in March 1890, becoming a professional entity. John H McLaughlin, John Glass and new member of the committee, Pat Welsh; were fully behind the proposal and saw potential in the professional game. On the other hand, Brother Walfrid viewed the idea in bad taste and saw breaking away from the roots of his club as a betrayal to its very foundations. Despite his resistance, the Hoops had entered the professional league by August. Ten thousand supporters showed up for the first Celtic, league match. It was a below par performance, culminating in a 4-1 defeat against Renton! This first process of the later switch in focus to football and business matters was not simple. Many official history books suggest that it was with great regret that the Club slowly reduced donations to 'The Poor Children's Dinner Table' and other charitable causes from 1892. They would support this by claiming that the circumstances surrounding Celtic at the time demanded that their stance on charity be realigned. Celtic was in the red and to continue donating to charity would be self-destructive. When broached on the issue, John Glass claimed: "Once the Club is in the clear it will be willing to assist charities in whatever way possible again." In opposition to this point, the Club had approved £100 for the treasurer. This approval rather contradictory for an institution rooted in charity! Though a somewhat conflict in rudiments, the size of Celtic FC may genuinely have been a factor in the Club's cessation of charitable donations though. Celtic faced intense competition from the constant emergence of more professional structures within other clubs. Additionally, strengthening the conviction that Celtic would not prosper in the amateur game, was the fact that administration and functional staff would simply not adhere to the notion of minimal pay; especially not when faced with the tough task of managing an increasingly popular entity. With that in mind, the topic was discussed at the 1897 AGM and the Club had become a limited company by way of democratic vote at the end of the meeting.

However, another theory on the early changes at the Club is disturbingly darker. This theory was written and kindly sent to me by Celtic history fanatic, Stephen Dennie, who had this article published in Celtic and political fanzine: 'TAL.'

Unfortunately, the early demise of the Celtic Football Club's intended charitable purposes, were due to the departure and appalling treatment of Brother Walfrid and like-minded board members. The people responsible for allowing personal power, greed and wealth, to eradicate the charitable notions that the Club proudly cherished; did so by forcing the Club to change into a Private limited company. They did this through the use of bullying tactics, quite readily, to gain their personal dreams of wealth and riches.

These members in question were led by John H McLaughlin. The decision was made in St. Mary's Hall on the 4th march 1897, when memberships voted for change. The Club wasn't even a decade old. Yet, as early as 1892 almost immediately after Brother Walfrid's departure, the Club's original charitable intentions seemed to be of little importance. (Thankfully they were upheld by the supporters. ←Added by me)

The new Celtic outlook deemed easily attainable profits, bonuses and huge salaries, the number one priority. Oh the irony (you decide) that their new lavish lifestyle was being mainly funded by the money generated from the poverty stricken Irish immigrants of Glasgow's east end, paying gate fees to watch Celtic play. Undoubtedly those same Irish immigrants that volunteered to build the new stadium would also have been paying an unreduced entrance fee to watch Celtic play as well.

The board members, had fans believe that an establishment of a limited liability company was the Club's natural evolution to paving the way for further progress, whilst no doubt claiming that if Celtic remained a purely charitable institution then they would have gone on to become an endearing eccentricity, in the manner of Queens Park.

In 1895 the Glasgow Observer ran a story condemning ' the biggest-drawing Club in Scotland', for not one penny had been donated to the Poor Children's Dinner Table, to which the Club had been instituted; even though the demand for free dinners had increased from sixty six thousand to ninety seven thousand in little over a year.

All the while players, committee members and officials of the Club had become so fixated and intent on fiddling money from the Club without declaration to anyone outside the board members, that by June 1895 twelve members of Celtic (players and officials) were listed as proprietors of public houses in Glasgow and Lanarkshire. The Club, which originated for charity (and still had many supporters carrying out charitable work←Added by me), *had turned into 'a gravy train' for certain individuals. A rather unholy alliance with the drink trade at the perceived expense of the Club's charitable remit was well and truly in place.*

In fact the Club's board of directors after turning Ltd, consisted of six wine and spirits merchants and a builders merchant (John Glass) or as I would have called it "six publicans- only one glass."

Brother Walfrid had the final remark for McLaughlin and co, when Celtic were returning from a continental tour in 1911. He parted from them in London with a farewell remark:
"Well, well. Time has brought changes. Outside ourselves there are a few left of the old brigade. It's good to see you all so well, and I feel younger with the meeting. Goodbye, God Bless you!"

<u>Timeline of the change at Celtic:</u>
[1889] Catholic charities received donation of £421 from the Club.

[1891] £545 of charitable donations made by the Club.

[1892] Brother Walfrid is transferred from the Club by his superiors to take up a post in London.

[1892] Only after he had departed could the advocates of

*limited liability and paid officials characterise their
opponents safely in such terms as 'impertinent meddlers',
'dinner table soreheads', and 'soup kitchen cranks'.*

*[1892] After Walfrids departure Charitable donations were
slashed to £230.*

[1895] No charitable donations made by Celtic.

*[1897] March 4th, Celtic AGM, results in the Club
becoming a Private Limited Company, and they paid
£10,000 to the landlord of the site of the stadium to have
full ownership of the land.*

Once the Club did turn in to a limited company, it was still
a fantastic one. It achieved great success. Crowds and funds
had exceeded all expectations. Unfortunately, the Club was
a victim of its accomplishments. The landlord had taken
note of the rising Celtic fortune. Rather iniquitously, he had
upstretched his rental demands from £50 to £450 per year.
Such elevation in costs would not be feasible. Therefore the
decision was made to relocate in the year of 1892. A local
journalist likened the relocation to 'moving from a
graveyard to paradise.' Thus the famous 'Paradise'
nickname for Celtic Park was adopted and has stuck with
supporters to the present day. The site selected was beside
Janefield Street Cemetery; the same position as the current
stadium.

Just as four years previously, volunteers were again
required to construct the new stadium. The site was a
disused brickyard, with a forty foot quarry half filled by
water. One hundred thousand cartloads of earth were used
to fill the crater after the water had been removed. The
Hoop's new site was designed in the shape of an oval.
Vast-terracing was also constructed. Freshly imported turf

was delivered from Donegal and laid by convicted Fenian and Irish politician, Michael Davitt, in the centre circle. That first sod of turf was commemorated with the following poem:

On alien soil like yourself I am here;
I'll take root and flourish, of that never fear;
And though I'll be crossed sore and oft by the foes,
You'll find me as hardy as Thistle or Rose.
Let your play honour me and my friend Michael Davitt.

Sadly, the turf was stolen that evening, but the Irish heart had been implemented at 'Paradise' already. Soon after 'Paradise's' opening, shamrocks were spotted growing around the centre circle. It is thought that this is the where the term and now current Club crest, 'four leaf clover' stems from.

By 1903, Celtic had changed from vertical green and white stripes, donned between the year of 1889 and 1903, to wearing the iconic hooped jersey that stays synonymous with the Club today.

However, decent advances to stadia were much slower. Problems first arose with the stadium when the disastrous seventy two feet tall Grant Stand was built in 1898. It required the road we now know as Kerrydale Street to be constructed, so that the huge gallery could link to London Road. The stand had a number of modifications made to it to try and overcome the issue of condensation. The fitted windows may have been a retardant to weather blemishes, but when the stand was full, they had an unfortunate tendency to steam up and prevent occupants from being able to see the match!

It was not until 1957 that each area of terracing had been covered. Even later, in 1959, the Club installed its first set of floodlights! Rumour has it that they towered at two hundred and eight feet tall – the largest set of floodlights in the world at that time. This fact is none too surprising though, for Celtic were the pioneers of floodlights in Britain, having attempted, albeit unsuccessfully, to light the stadium for an evening encounter with Clyde on Christmas day as far back as 1897!

Despite its problems, Celtic Park was always a popular venue in the sporting domain; hosting the fifth World Cycling Championships in 1897, world champion boxer's bouts from 1917 and staging a British and European title fight in 1949. Other elite events held at the ground included the first official British Speedway meeting in 1928 and a Pedestrianism joust between the English and American champions in 1896! (Pedestrianism was an extremely dull sport, involving lengthily walks that sometimes lasted a full day before one walker prevailed as victor!)

All of this history would not be able to be retold, at least authentically, had a fire at 'Paradise' been ever so slightly more extensive! After a small stand fire in 1904, damage to the Pavillion side of the stadium had been repaired. However, in May 1929 the job was finished when Celtic Park befell further bad luck and caught ablaze. Construction workers architecting a new South Stand quickly raised the alarm but the speed of the fire meant that the wooden Pavilion could not be saved. Stowed in the building, were the early photographs and documentation from the first forty years of the Club. Everything but a safe was destroyed. The safe, of which all hopes hinged on the contents of, had been damaged having struck a radiator as it fell from the above floor. Thankfully, the Club's early records of charitable contributions and committee men were found inside, in good condition. They had survived and allow us to tell the Celtic story.

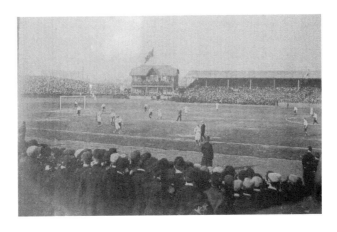

Celtic fans at Celtic Park in 1894 – Image donated from Jamie Fox's collection

Statue of Brother Walfrid outside Celtic Park – Image courtesy of Jamie Fox

What the Club Means & Represents

There are many Celtic fans from each walk of life and in every corner of the globe. Within that huge scale, this individual piece is dedicated to my personal view on what Celtic means and represents. Bear with me; I will delve into entries from the wider fan base in due course!

I am told that my affinity with Celtic Football Club really began at the age of four years old. I was totally besotted with football and the time for selecting my supporting path had come. In truth the decision was made easy as I was heavily drawn towards Celtic and Ireland throughout my short life. I had been dressed in a Hoops kit at birth and laid in the centre of an Irish tri-colour. Inevitably I chose to follow the green and white jersey that was so familiar to me, totally unaware that this would prove such an excellent decision.

My earliest notable memories of the Club are from the beginning of the 2002/2003 season. I used to go to the house of my dear friend and neighbour, Pete Duffy, with my dad to watch the games. Pete grew up in the Gorbals and stood on the old terracing of the Celtic End, having graduated from the Rangers End as a child. He attended most games both home and away from 1956 until his move down south in 1983. An 'uber-Celt', he became my tutor in all matters Celtic and I, his eager protégé.

My abiding memory of the Club is of the passion, the sea of green and white and the volume of supporters that followed Celtic around Europe that season. However, my initial experience of what it truly means to follow this Club came to fruition in March of 2003. Dad and I had acquired two tickets in the Main Stand at Anfield for the UEFA Cup Quarter-Final clash between Liverpool and Celtic. A packed stadium sent a tingle down my spine with a heartfelt rendition of the shared anthem, 'You'll Never Walk Alone.' With the game drawing to its conclusion, the travelling fans were sent into delirium as John Hartson struck a thunderbolt beyond the reach of Liverpool goalkeeper, Jerszy Dudek. We were through!

After seeing off Boavista, I was desperate to get tickets for the final in Seville. Only a disastrous mistake, which remains a sore point, prevented me from going. A few days after the final, my mum's cousin (Paul) came round our house to visit. He was over from Spain and you guessed it, he lived in Seville. It is important to stress that Dad and I did not know Paul very well at this time. Mum did. All was well until Paul spotted my Celtic shirt and proceeded to open the lid of his laptop. Dad and I looked to our horror as he loaded picture after picture of his view from the Celtic support at the UEFA Cup Final. My heart sank when Paul said: "I got tickets weeks ago through work. I could have got them easy if your mum had told me that you were Celtic fans!"

Despite the 2002/2003 season ending without a trophy, nothing could detract from the monumental achievements of O'Neill and his squad. I was lucky to be brought up in that era and from that point my interest in the Club grew.

Personally speaking, I feel that Celtic renders the values of much that is good within society. It is my view that the Club holds/held five main facets: A Scottish based Club with strong Irish heritage and culture, social inclusion, charitable endeavour, a desire to achieve footballing excellence (known as the Celtic way) and incredible support. Other factors include: a Club steeped in history, a support full of banter and a family unity. Sadly, I feel forced to omit the desire for footballing excellence from my impressive list these days. I plead that this is due to a huge cut in transfer budget, largely necessary because of the prohibitive financial environment of Scottish football.

The same cannot be said when it comes to charity. I have such clarity in this regard because of the incredibly good nature in which many Celtic fans have always contributed to worthy causes. This is done through (UK record breaking) food banks, donations and self-organised events. Though my previous chapter indicates a loss of these principles at boardroom level in 1897, the recovery of these ideals in the decades that followed has been very pleasing. It would be wrong of me to not allude to the fact that the creation of 'Celtic FC Foundation' has been a very positive element of the Club. There is no doubting that the range of different initiatives and financial assistance, provided by the Foundation, have been appreciated at local, national and international levels. Through their genuine altruism, the Foundation has helped some two and a half million people to date. The level of charitable action carried out by the Club is staggering. I am hard pressed to think of anywhere else that a match like John Kennedy's testimonial, full of retired players, could attract a crowd of sixty thousand people. That game ultimately enabled the Foundation to feed, water and save over sixty six thousand victims of famine in East Africa! That is just one of many examples that show the maintenance of our roots. Ensuring that the founder's visions stay undiminished is something that is rightfully promoted and that we can all be proud of.

It is certainly the off field aspects of Celtic which engender in me the deepest emotions of adoration and pride. It is these emotions that manifest themselves within individual supporters and transmit to the field of play. Tommy Burns epitomised this point when referring to the sacred hooped shirt. He stated: "When you pull on that jersey you are playing for a people and a cause." It is this fact that has helped to create much success throughout the Club's history and contributed to the previously upheld aim of achieving footballing excellence throughout the years.

I also believe that we have the finest of traditions. This is exemplified by our policy of social inclusion. We have a range of fans from various races, religions, creeds and colour, all welcomed into the Celtic family. When Celtic fans meet, there is a common bond found in our unique community spirit and every chance that they'll become friends for life. Having an association with the Club was described in the following way by Giorgios Samaras: "The atmosphere here at Celtic is really like a family, everybody is so welcoming when you are a part of the Club." This family bond is matched by few other clubs, a relationship that is created by a unity in beliefs and passion far beyond supporting a football team. Three examples of this relationship have been at the fore in recent seasons. They are the unanimous backing of Neil Lennon, John Hartson and Stiliyan Petrov in their respective times of extreme difficulty.

The sense of equality found in the family like support is a core value of the Club. To those that pledge allegiance to the Celtic badge; nobody is inferior or otherwise. This is supported by Bill Shankly when he said: "Celtic is like a form of socialism." The general implementation of such principles and political sympathies within the Celtic support, explains the various anti-racist, anti-fascist and left wing figure head banners that can be seen in the stands to this day. It is of course up to each supporter to educate themselves about global political matters and assume their own opinion. But the general persuasion amongst the fans has meant that the Club has always been known for its stance against injustice and to speak out for the oppressed. In recent times, the emergence of the Green Brigade has carried this further, to the voicing of support for the anti-fascist organisations: 'Alerta Network' and the 'Antifa Movement'.

Another, perhaps more recent facet is exemplary fan conduct. I am enabled to take immense pride in the reputation of the Celtic fans throughout Europe. Celtic followers regularly mix peacefully with opposing supporters and very rarely incite trouble. The most famous example of this was at the UEFA Cup Final in Seville when eighty thousand Hoops fans descended on the city. Heavy alcohol consumption, coupled with heart-breaking defeat, would lead most supports to behave badly. Not a single arrest was made in Seville, a testament to the Club and its values.

In terms of national identities, there is a clear dualism. Whilst the Club has integrated into Scottish society, there are incredibly strong ties to Ireland as well. In addition to clearly connected points in my previous chapter, Celtic also attracts a big support, or at least affection from a number of people living in the thirty two counties of the Emerald Isle. Many fans both Scottish based and globally, hail from Irish descent as well, meaning that the heritage and culture of the country is very much alive at Celtic Park today.

A combination of the fact that Eire was under total occupation at the time of Celtic's formation and that Celtic fans were discriminated against in Scotland (mirroring the oppressive hardships endured in Ireland); meant a support for Irish Republicanism took centre stage. As the situation in Scotland and particularly the north of Ireland has greatly improved, that has begun to wane. Yet there are still underlying sympathies, many of which are voiced in pubs, concert halls and by the away support.

Songs including the 'Fields of Athenry' and 'Let the People Sing' are the musical foundation of Irish identity and rebellion. They are of great meaning to me. These songs are not sectarian, as often alleged by those who do not understand the faithful. Instead, they protest the injustices that both the Irish back home and the diaspora worldwide have had to endure. Furthermore, they commemorate those that fought and died in the name of independence, justice and equality. The militant nature of those sometimes referenced was not based upon religion, but rather a desire to free their native land from the oppressor!

The Irish-Scot constituent of the support has meant that since the Club's inception many other Folk, Rebel and Celtic songs could be heard and created. These songs celebrate and express culture at the same time as giving vocal support to the team. Celtic is perhaps the only football club in the world that can boast such a unique musical tradition. Our songs are special in the sense that very few clubs have such a number with verse and chorus. Even fewer witness such an evolution of their songbook and fewer still have songs with such history, celebration and social relevance behind them. Such songs range from purely football related matters, (Willie Maley and

Hampden in the sun) to wider social contexts, ('Viva La Quinta Brigada' and 'This Land Is Your Land') which much of the support relates to. Times change, the repertoire adapts but the musical tradition is always maintained.

The oral celebration and pride of our roots has led to many other factors that shape Celtic as a Club. It is fair to say that we have always been an underdog. Yet as a sizeable minority, Celtic has remained unbowed and unbroken. Until recent, in my view, the SFA had operated in a partial manner against the Club for this reason. Thus time and again our teams have had to dig deep to overcome adversity. This characteristic has been utilised many times such as coming back from losing positions late on in games. We never give up!

Such passion and spirit makes for an incomparable atmosphere at Celtic Park on European nights, derby matches and amongst the massive hardcore away support. Wherever Celtic goes you can be sure that there will be a huge travelling support in tow. Be it across the border in England or across the world in Australia. A European tie or a pre-season friendly.

Finally, Celtic has presented me with a basic guide for my life. It has taught me moralities through enjoyment with like-minded and enthusiastic people.

Different segments of the Club's ethos are taken on by many Celtic fans, as we stand together, united as one.

The first and longest serving manager in our history, Willie Maley, so brilliantly describes my overriding thoughts: "The Club has been my life and I feel without it my existence would be empty indeed."

What Celtic means & represents to the wider fan base:

This section enables the diverse representations of the Club to be displayed from an equally diverse support. Some entries synopsize Celtic in a word, others opt for longer contributions. The common aura is one of unquestionable passion.

I guess I would conclude that Celtic is my moral compass which encapsulates and defines how I view the world around me. We were born from the vision of a man who wanted to improve the lives of the poor in the east end of Glasgow with a message that resonates with every right minded person no matter gender, creed or colour. Our reason for existence is internationalist and football is merely the means by which we love and carry the message, which explains why we are welcomed in virtually every domain that we visit. More than a club in every sense!
(Jim)

As a youngster of about 8-9 years old I used to sit and listen to my uncles David & Lawrence talking about the football scores of that day. When it came to the Celtic result whether it was a win, lose or draw there was no doubting that both these men loved this football club. They would regale about the times they went to watch them, the players that they saw and also the journey to and from the games. Our family stayed over on the east coast of Scotland in Fife and some folk would say it was strange that my uncles and their friends would support a team that was on the other side of the country, especially when there were a number of teams closer to home that they could go and support.

After listening to numerous stories of their escapades I asked "when can I come and see The Famous Glasgow Celtic?" My uncle David then said he would take me to the upcoming game against Dundee Utd at Tannadice. I went running down our street to where my house was and excitedly told my mum that I was getting taken to a Celtic game by my Uncle David.

"No f*****g way," was her response to me. My uncle David was a bit of a drinker and my mum did not trust him to take me, a 10 year old boy, anywhere never mind to a football game.

I was in bits walking back up our street to my grans house at the top of the road to tell him I wasn't allowed. "Leave it with me Steven, I'll sort it out," he said. Now I don't know what he said to my mum but all of a sudden I was allowed to go to the football.

The game was only days away and it was all I could talk about. The Nuns that taught me at school had to keep telling me to shut up talking about it as I was telling everyone in class. As the day drew nearer, the excitement built day by day, the Friday night before the game I couldn't sleep it was like Christmas Eve, but eventually the day arrived. I was up out of my bed at the crack of dawn washed dressed and ready to go. My uncle arrived to collect me and when he did, mum told him in no uncertain terms to look after me and that if anything happened to me he was a dead man.

So out the house we went heading to the train station for the twenty minute train journey over the Tay Bridge to Dundee. On the way down through our town we popped into my uncle's local where he was meeting up with the others who were making the trip too. The Station Hotel had only just opened the doors at 11.00am and already there were loads of punters in, some going to the football, some not. Being a 10 year old, I wasn't allowed to be seen in the bar so I was shunted into the lounge bar that wasn't open at this time of day, with a glass of cola and poke of salt 'n' vinegar crisps. I'm just itching to get over and see the football. After what seemed an eternity to me but was only probably about an hour, we were off heading the short distance to the train station, on the train, and we're on our way to the football.

Once in Dundee, our group made a number of stops at boozers on the way up to Tannadice, every time I'm getting left outside to wait on them. Then, as we get to the top of the Hilltown, we can see the floodlights of Dens Park which is just up the road from Tannadice. We make our way down the road and turn the corner, there it is, Tannadice and more importantly inside is the Famous Glasgow Celtic. Back in those days it was just pay at the gate. So we are edging closer and closer to the turnstiles then BOOM we're in heading up the stone stairs and into the stadium.

It was already a mass of green and white. My uncle took me down the front behind the goal and told me to stay there and he would collect me at full time. The Celtic team are warming up and I'm almost within touching distance of Pat Bonner. All of a sudden one of the training balls is heading my way. I lean over to pick it up and all I hear is "Over here wee man," I look up to see who is shouting and standing right in front of me is none other than Roy Aitken.

I froze just staring up at this man "C'mon lad chuck the ball," he says and then I come to my senses and throw him the ball.

I'm in dream land, here are the players that I have pictures of on my bedroom wall running about right in front of me. I'm totally hooked now and the game hasn't even started.

The teams disappear back up the tunnel and there's a bit of a lull in the noise, a wee bit later the teams come out and there is an explosion of noise and colour from the Celtic support, who are behind the goal and stretch all the way round to the halfway line. The Celtic support breaks out into song and the flags and scarves are getting waved about. I'm totally mesmerised by this and I actually miss the kick off. (This won't be the first time I ever miss a kick off but latterly it's due to me sitting in the pub too long.)

Celtic won the game 3-1. I think Davie Provan, Murdo Mcleod and Brain Mclair scored the goals that day. At full time my uncle came and got me and we headed back towards the train station, again stopping at one or two pubs on the way back down. Eventually we got on the train to head home but that wasn't the last of the excitement for this day. After all the refreshment stops at the boozers my uncle was well on his way. At our stop he and his mates all jumped off the train forgetting about me as I had my head stuck into the programme not even noticing that they had got off until I heard this banging on the window and there was my uncle running along the platform as the train pulled out of the station. Here's me at 10 years old on this train all alone wondering what I was going to do. I didn't have to wonder too long as at the next station the station master got on and took me off the train. My uncle, even in his drunken state, had the savvy to get the guard at our town to phone ahead and get me off at the next stop, where one of my uncle's mate's wife came and collected me.

To this day, and I'm in my 40s now, my mum still doesn't know that my uncle David almost lost me on the short train journey from Dundee to Fife and more importantly my first ever Celtic game.

From that day on I was hooked on Glasgow Celtic, it was just the noise the colour the fans round about me who I never knew from Adam looking out for me, that made that day special for me. For me that is why this club that we all love is so special, it's been said before, that this is more than just a football club, it's a family, a way of life to hundreds of thousands of people around the world and why it is so special to every single one of us.

I now have a son who is only months old but there will come a time when he is old enough and my wife will probably say the very same thing to me that my mum said to my uncle David, but I will still take my 'Bhoy' to see "THE FAMOUS GLASGOW CELTIC" and he too will become a member of this very special Celtic family.
(Dickie)

My love of Celtic all started innocuously enough… In 2010 I ordered a few Celtic tops on eBay, but the tops never came and I emailed the seller to see when they were posted. He returned the email the next day and said there was an error with the address he put on the package and he had to re-post the package. As an apology, he included a signed picture of the Lisbon Lions in the box with the tops.

After I had received the package, he sent me back an email that asked if I was a Celtic supporter. My answer to him was that I had heard of Henrik Larsson, but that was it. I had no idea who was on the picture of the Lisbon Lions. This guy from eBay then proceeded to invite me to be introduced to all of his friends in Port Glasgow, who are also Celtic supporters on Facebook and provided me with links to The Celtic Wiki, where I could read up about the history of the Club.

At the same time there were two other issues that were simultaneously taking place. First, my children had started asking me to take them back to Mass at our local Catholic Church, where they had attended grade school. As we started to go on the weekends I was home, I found it very satisfying to go back to church as a family activity. Meanwhile, my then girlfriend had introduced me to her favorite show on Showtime, 'The Tudors', which is about King Henry VIII. At the time I didn't know the entire story and I am not treating the Showtime version as a walk through history as much as I am treating it as an awakening to go and search for the history of 'Bloody Mary' and England's move towards the Protestant faith.

With the confluence of all this information I started reading everything I could get my hands on about Celtic FC and Rangers FC. All the paranoia comments made by supporters on all the news stories featured on 'News Now' started to make sense. As I started to stream matches live in the fall of 2011, I could certainly tell there were two different sets of rules for each team. As an avid American sports viewer, the thought of one sided officials was foreign to me. But, it was plain as day and happening right in front of my eyes.

The first time I remembered this happening was when I was watching a Rangers match against Hearts and with the score tied, the fourth official showed four minutes of added time; in a match with no injuries, a few substitutions and no goals in the second half! Of course Rangers scored on a dodgy free kick - awarded in the fourth minute of added time. I can still hear myself screaming "The game is over already, blow the f*****g whistle," and can recall exactly where I was on the day!

From that point on, I was hooked! A few weeks later, the same guy that I purchased the tops from, had invited me to a game in Glasgow as his guest. I accepted as it became a goal of mine to see this spectacle for my own eyes!

As I emerged from the arrivals terminal in Glasgow in December 2011, there were two cars and four men that I'd never met before, waiting for me. From there, the trip kicked off with a wee bevy at their local, Donnachie's Pub in Port Glasgow. Since I had interacted with most of them on Facebook, there was this 'semi' familiar feeling; as if I had been friends with all these people my entire life. I was welcomed with open arms from the first minute! (To this day, Donnachie's is still my favorite place in Scotland to get a pint.)

The next night was my first game and it was Motherwell at Celtic Park. I remember thinking that we were having our own 'Green Street' moment, with twenty of us on the train into Glasgow and then down the Gallowgate to have a pint in all the places I had only read about or seen pictures of: including Bar 67 and Baird's. That night I was lucky enough to get a ticket in section 111. Yes, a Yank standing with the Green Brigade! Paddy McCourt scored the only goal of the game. I can still feel the hair on my neck stand up when he scored and the whole stadium started chanting "Paddy McCourt's Fenian Army!"

A few days later a new mate, Kevin Cushnahan, found a way to get two tickets to Ibrox for the New Year's Glasgow Derby. It was an introduction to 'The Supporter's Bus', as compared to the American tradition of tailgating. To be segregated and escorted to the stadium created an odd feeling outside the stadium. I could sense the tension of Ranger's supporters chanting across the line of police dressed in high-visibility yellow jackets. But once inside it was magical. We witnessed a Samaras brace and I still have my personal video of the penalty kick that he put past McGregor as a keepsake. On the bus on the way home I was considered their lucky charm and serenaded by the members of the Port Glasgow Emerald Celtic Supporters Club. WHAT A DAY!!!

From that point on, I was infected with the Celtic bug and realised right then that Celtic may not be my first love (NY Yankees claim that accolade), but because of the supporter's passion, community connection and what the Club stood for, Celtic would be my deepest and longest lasting love.

As time went on, I became even more connected to my new mates, through using Skype and chatting on Facebook. I'd even get video calls from the supporter's bus as they started singing 'The Holy Doctor' song while on road trips to see Celtic play. But, Celtic lost the title that year to Rangers and after Neil Lennon was attacked at Tynecastle, I knew I had to get back to Glasgow as soon as possible. I remember feeling like I wanted to cry as Lennon addressed the crowd and said "This isn't the end. It's just the beginning."

That next fall, I made it to Tynecastle (the scene of the crime) but the Hoops lost that day after Commons was given a straight red card. Once again, the bus was absolutely rocking with songs and filled to the entire ride with large amounts of Buckfast, El Dorado, Jagermeister, lager and Strongbow. Or so the pictures reminded me…

The trip was made even better as I was able to combine it with a christening ceremony for one of my new found friends. That day was one of my proudest as I was called a 'Tim'. I don't know why, but it never crossed my mind because I always thought of myself as an outsider. That night I remember sitting in Donnachie's (AGAIN) and just watching everything around me thinking 'How the f**k did I get here?' I knew the people, their kids, and their spouses as if I was always there and never gone.

Flash forward another eighteen months. My wife and I have been to a wedding, a Cup Final at Hampden for the loss to 'Killie' and back to Celtic Park to get a tour of Parkhead. My wife, for Christmas, bought me a brick with my name on it that resides on the Tommy Burns Wall. We've even taken trips to New York to see friends on their honeymoon and will travel to Florida for friends who will be vacationing there this summer!

As if that wasn't enough, I decided to start my own Celtic Supporters Club, the Myrtle Beach Bawdeep CSC. If you wondered where the name came from, I can give you one guess. Yes, my 'Bhoys' from the Port Glasgow Emerald CSC convinced me to go with the word that John Rodgers always just blurts out (for some reason it just feels as if the only thing he ever says is 'Bawdeep' as if he has Tourette's syndrome).

Now we have club pins, a Facebook page and a twitter account. But, the best part is the Club stickers that I had made. If someone asks me for a few, I send them out no matter where they are as long as they promise to post a picture of the sticker. To my knowledge, they're on cars in Massachusetts, Michigan and South Carolina. They're also pictures of the stickers in bars from Glasgow to California, to Alaska, to Dublin, to Vegas, to Mexico. So far the best picture I've seen is the one of The Bawdeep CSC in the National Stadium in Lisbon right below where Billy McNeill stood with the trophy in 1967! (Oh and I think I remember once seeing a picture of a Bawdeep CSC sticker on the wall of 'Castle Gresyskull').

What a fun filled ride it has been. And, as Celtic prepares to take possession of the SPL trophy, all I can think of is when I will get back to Paradise again to see Celtic. But, even more importantly to see virtual friends made by mistake that have become a real part of my life and left an indelible impression on me.

Always remember that WE Tims are everywhere! And as the Myrtle Beach Bawdeep CSC motto goes... 'Faithful through and through, no matter where in the world we are,'
*(**John Davila- Myrtle Beach Bawdeep CSC**)*

After sending this story to me, John kept in touch. I then had the pleasure of meeting him in London and we keep in contact regularly. In 2013, John directed me to his friends in Port Glasgow, who helped me with match tickets for

Celtic v Ajax. I am now close friends with the Port Glasgow Emerald CSC members, who have arranged tickets on other big European nights and have shared a number of fantastic moments with me. Like John, we keep in contact regularly. It is things like that, which make writing this book the best thing that I have ever done.

John (fat Kelvin Wilson) and Port Glasgow Emerald CSC members. If you want to hear more from John, you can tune into his 'Smell the Glove' podcast on Hail Hail Media.

In short, Celtic is a symbol and embodiment of a vision of progression.
(Henry Watham)

It's very cliché, but Celtic means literally everything. Not a day passes by where my thoughts aren't totally consumed by the Club. Supporting Celtic is a way of life in itself. It's like a relationship, but a relationship that lasts forever, and a relationship that no other thing on the planet can make you go through the same amount of emotions as. The Club has given me some of the happiest, saddest and craziest days of my life, and I've loved every one of them!
(Jordon)

Celtic is a Scottish Club with Irish connections, a Club for all people and cultures, a Club that wants to play football the way it should be played, backed by fans that live and breathe green and white.
(Jamie McLaughlin)

This is what Celtic as a club means to me, it's not my opinion on what it should mean to anyone else or that because of my faith, political views or general personality, I feel that all Celtic fans should take the mould of my opinions. My heart swells with pride knowing that Celtic is a club loved by all creed, colour and race.

Celtic for me is an Irish club that plays in Glasgow; it is a symbol of the Irish and indeed Irish Republicanism in the city. It is also Catholic, primarily but not solely or discriminately, which is undeniable through its origin. It is also a club loved and despised equally worldwide, due to its supporter's sympathies to those who live in tyranny and oppression and their stance on any form of discrimination to any other human being. The reasons I feel this are many.

Celtic firstly for me has the distinction of playing on foreign soil. It is an Irish club playing in Scotland, and represents the Irish Diaspora who existed when the club was formed, and who exist in this country still through their children, grandchildren and so on. This also accounts for the large support, which travels over from Ireland on a weekly basis. In the early days they may have had family in Glasgow who told them about this wonderful club and what it represents to the Irish community in Glasgow. This love of the Club again was passed down the generations growing up in Ireland, who were born into the Celtic tradition. In the occupied six counties in Ireland, those who didn't know of Celtic through family or friends soon heard of this Club over the sea, whose fans waved the Irish tri-colour and sang the songs of the struggle they were living. Some of these supporters where in Republican Flute Bands that came over for marches to support them, and told them about the Club and invited them to matches, and they fell in love too.

The Club's first patron was Michael Davitt, a former Fenian and the founder of the National Land League. He visited Celtic Park several times to enthusiastic receptions in his role. In March 1892 he laid the first sod at the new Celtic Park, a piece of turf from Donegal containing shamrocks. He was not the only politician to visit Celtic Park, T. D. Sullivan, was met by the Club and cheered by the players and fans and returned the favour with a verse of his song, which served as the Irish national anthem for over 50 years, 'God Save Ireland', a song which remembers the Manchester martyrs.

These facts and many more prove that geography doesn't dictate nationality. This is an Irish club in Scotland.

That leads me onto the supporters. The reason the Club's fans are open to all people of the world, for me, stems from the fact the Club is Irish and the Irish Republican supporters the Club has. This is due, not only to the solidarity the Republican movement has with struggles worldwide, which leads to education of other people's plights and belief's. It is also due to the fact that the Club was set up by and for immigrants who were persecuted and racially abused when they arrived in this country due to their race and religion. This abuse was pivotal in ensuring that Celtic supporters realise that those suffering any form of bigotry today, are suffering what they and their ancestors did, and still do, for being Irish or Catholic or both.

This and a lot more culminates in a club that for me is special in so many ways. It also brings together a group of supporters who have lived under a certain amount of persecution, due to their faith, political and social beliefs or just the fact they support Celtic. This common bond unites the support with pride that we have a successful symbol for us all, i.e. Celtic Football Club, to follow, come what may and to show pride in who and what we are: Celtic supporters.

All of the above is personal opinion and is not what I deem a Celtic supporter has to be or feel.
(JPlough)

Interview with Damien Quinn (formerly lead singer of Justice Band)

Q) What do you think Celtic Football Club represents and what do you think that the support stands for?

A) Celtic Football Club represents the Irish people around the world. You have to go back to the beginning when Brother Walfrid's purpose was to set up a football team to raise funds for the children of Irish families living in the east end of Glasgow. So this was the foundation of an organisation ready to help the Irish people living there that were already discriminated against by the authorities as no jobs were being offered to the Irish that had settled there apart from low paid ones in harsh conditions.

Most of the Irish people and their families flooded into the likes of Glasgow seeking a better life after the famine in the 1840s. So people saw the idea of Brother Walfrid's Celtic as a lifeline for the Irish in Scotland. It allowed the Irish to become part of Scotland and give them an identity there and it also gives people born in Scotland to Irish parents a connection to Ireland. So people must always look back to reasons behind the formation of the Club.

The support stands for each and every Irish person that was forced to leave Ireland after the famine and settle in Scotland, especially Glasgow and not forgetting the ideals of Brother Walfrid and what he achieved in the formation of the Club.

In the modern day, this can be lost and forgot about by the PLC, especially with all the money that the games command now. But this is the change in all football throughout the world.

Q) What does being a Celtic fan mean to you?

A) Being a Celtic fan gives you a great sense of pride in being part of one big family, a pride that feels the greatest on European match nights. When you wear a Celtic top you are displaying this pride to everyone around and also remembering all the great Celtic legends that have passed on.

Q) What is the best gig that you have ever performed in front of Celtic fans?

A) The best gig has to be the Celtic Convention that was held in Santa Ponsa in 2010. Upwards of 1,200 Celtic fans from around the world gathered every night in the Spanish Square for the nightly concerts organised by a great man, Harry Flynn, owner of The Celts Well Inn. I had the pleasure of opening the convention by being the first act on stage and I did a few gigs throughout the festival. Then, after each concert, I would play in the Celts Well Inn until the early hours of the morning.

The atmosphere was electric and it turned out to be an amazing festival with people to this day always enquiring if there will be another one happening. The amount of friends that I have made in the Celtic community is huge and they will always be friends for life. But the best Celtic minded venue to play at anywhere in the world has to be the famous Barrowlands in Glasgow. I did a few support gigs there before 'The Wolfe Tones', to a crowd of two thousand people. This was the best experience ever in my music career and to think of the amount of famous people that have stood on that stage in the past and performed for many thousands of people is excellent. It's also a favourite venue for many of the Celtic supporters.

Q) Do you think that the political music culture will always be a part of the support?

A) Republicanism and Rebel music will always be a part of the Celtic culture. On match days you will always hear sections of the crowds singing Rebel songs including 'Boys of the Old Brigade', 'Roll Of Honour', 'Aiden McAnespie' etc. Singing Rebel songs at these matches form some sort of camaraderie among the fans and also bring an atmosphere to any stadium. But I am sure that members of the board would rather that they were not sung. And even the police in Glasgow are trying stamp it out around the pubs there.

You also have to go back to the history of the formation of the Club when Brother Walfrid attended the home of Willie Maley's family to enlist help in setting up Glasgow Celtic. One of the men he brought with him was a Fenian by the name of Pat Welsh, who was wanted in Ireland by the police, who said he was a terrorist.

It was Willie Maley's father, who was in the British Army in Ireland, that let Pat Welsh get onto the boat to come to Scotland to live. He turned a blind eye when he recognised him as he knew if he handed him over that he would be executed. So a Republican was actually one of the founding members along with Brother Walfrid, who got the ball rolling when it came to set up Celtic. I am also proud of the fact that Willie Maley was born in my hometown of Newry Co. Down; the man that made Celtic.

In the last few decades more and more Republicans have started to attend Celtic matches. The new era of peace has allowed for this and given Republicans something else to pump the adrenalin. They took to travelling to Scotland and attending Celtic games, socialising in the east end of Glasgow and getting to enjoy themselves; whilst also singing Rebel Songs at Celtic Park.

I remember attending games with many Republicans and many of them had never previously been at Celtic Park but now they were part of the Celtic family. But, there were also many arrests and delays at Stranraer Port because of people's connections to the Republican Movement.

I remember when travelling over with our family band JUSTICE, we would always be stopped and harassed, but one incident I still remember is when we were travelling home in two cars. My late brother Dessie was driving in front and we were pushing for time to make the sailing. When we got to the port of Stranraer, the Police were waiting and they asked Dessie for his licence. When they saw the name 'D.Quinn' they just waved him into the side to proceed with a full search, while waving us on through. Even though Dessie had absolutely no interest in Republicanism, just because he shared the same initial of his first name with me, this action was taken against him. He missed the sailing and didn't get home until the next day.

Even after the ceasefire was in place, you still had to face the wrath of the police at the docks in Stranraer, which meant you were often arrested and questioned and in a lot of cases you missed the sailing back home. This still continues today. In a recent incident I was the only car held in Cairnryan, which is the new port that you sail into. While travelling to a weekend of gigs in Scotland, they held me for over two hours for questioning and kept my iPhone. I didn't receive it until I was returning on the Monday, which meant I was late for the first night's gig and I also had no contact with the organisers of the other gigs.

In my eyes there will always be people who are Republicans that will continue to follow the Famous Glasgow Celtic and sing the Rebel Songs.

Q) Lastly, would it be fair to say that the Celtic support still side with the oppressed (outside of the Irish)?

A) I would have no doubt in saying that the majority of Celtic supporters are anti-imperialist and anti-monarchist. The support for the people of Scotland to have their own Independence is strengthening and the latest Westminster Elections returned a massive vote for the SNP here in 2015. I also have no doubt that the majority of the Celtic support also stands in solidarity with the people of the six Counties in their desire for there to be a United Ireland as well.

'This Celtic Football Club is much more than a football club. To a lot of people it's a way of life.'
(Michael)

I remember as a kid with zero football knowledge, telling my dad I was a Dundee fan. He looked disappointed, so I asked which team he supported. To which he replied "Celtic." So I decided to support them (even though I thought 'Celtic' was a silly name my dad made up!) I started getting seriously into football in '86 and by the time my dad took me to my first game (3-2 defeat at Tannadice) I was hooked. My first trip to Parkhead was a 0-0 draw with the dons but the journey, walk up the Gallowgate, burger vans and electric buzz of the crowd at the old ground will never leave me. In my teens I tagged along with mates to a good few Dundee games but once a Tim, always a Tim; it's just something that you are. The arrival of Fergus probably reignited my passion and for the last twenty years I have followed them faithfully, be that through TV, radio, the odd match or a season ticket.

Celtic represent where my family came from, Ireland, and where the Irish in Scotland are now. They represent charity, triumphs, tragedies and ultimately success. Only someone who loves Celtic truly gets it. The Celtic story parallels my own story in a way, formed to provide help to people like my ancestors. My family then integrated into Scottish society, as did Celtic, who are now a Scottish institution with proud Irish links and global appeal. I think Rod Stewart said the stadium, the hoops, the history; the whole story just gets into your soul. That sums it up for me. Culture and society has changed since the Club was formed but Celtic must always adapt, strive to address whatever new issues society throws up, reach out to as many people as possible; whilst staying true to our roots and using these roots to positively promote the name of Celtic FC.

(Jungletones)

It's in the blood. I was born into a Celtic fanatic family. In fact, my old lady thought she was going into labour, in the south stand, after the seventh goal at Hampden, when we cuffed the Huns 7-1, back in '57. That was me jumping for joy. My folks took us 3 kids to all the home games and some of the away ones too, like Firhill and Shawfield ... my Dad drove the Celtic Supporters Club double decker from Benny's Bar on the NW corner of Gorbals Cross. 'Wonder if anyone else remembers that joint? When I lived down under, me and my sister set the alarm at daft o'clock, to tune into the BBC World Service, to hear what the score was. I've been south of the border now for over twenty years. I don't get to many games these days but even just watching Celtic online is like coming home. It strikes a chord somewhere deep in my soul. I'm sure we all find it hard to imagine life without Celtic in it. When Celtic take to the field, I feel the greatest emotion of joy. To me, they are not playing another team for points or trophies, but playing for the cause, a cause which bonds us all together, from rock stars to Hollywood actors, from the children of the east end to the children of Thailand, no other club kindles the fires within you like Celtic. To explain it in words is impossible, you just have to live it.

(Molly)

For me the essence of Celtic has its origins clearly in the Irish immigrant - the unifying battle of the underdog. To be a Celtic fan is to follow a righteous path of fair play, which has a magnetic effect to others. Our experiences as the children of immigrants, has taught us to be thankful for we ourselves, and stand for the struggle of the weak & oppressed. This is why today; the fans have a strong social conscious manifest in our diverse following, the righteous & vocal backing of Irish unity, and anti-fascism to name but a few. We would never, for example, accommodate religious bias in our culture like our horrible neighbours; in fact we self-police our behaviour. What's different about sides like Barcelona is that their stances are just embodied in their sponsorship of UNICEF!

(Gavin)

When I first met my ex-girlfriend she knew firsthand how much the Club meant to me. About a month before the UEFA Cup Final, I thought like every other Celtic fan that I would not reach a ticket... she gave me an ultimatum, 'go to the final and we are no longer in a relationship and our marriage plans are no longer either!' I went to the final and went to the North American tour as well. I guess that's how much the Club means to me. The ex-girlfriend is still ex, and I'm now married with a baby on the way.

(Ronald White)

Celtic, my Celtic, in my thoughts and in my prayers from morning till night. From cradle days it is passed on from generation to each new born. To walk along the Gallowgate to Celtic park, hear the songs, see the colours, feel the pride of wearing the hoops, the feeling of something inside so strong. Many people try to put into words what it is to be a Celtic fan, I can't, just that I am blessed to be one of you, and that my son and daughters, and grandchildren are one of you too. God bless the Celtic.

(Papabee)

The rollercoaster of emotions that Celtic has put me through over the years easily puts the Club on par with everything that's important to me. The highs of going to the home of the former Rangers FC and winning and having tears of joy, to feeling so deflated when great men such as Tommy Burns and Phil O'Donnell passed, are times when the unity of the fans really gave me a lump in the throat. I've used a lot of words during these paragraphs giving examples of what Celtic means to me, but you can never really explain it, it's one of those situations where only another fellow supporter knows the exact feelings you have. Feelings you can't always put into words. I love the Club and football would not be the same without Celtic for me.

(Mercercelt)

If I could bottle how I feel every time that Celtic score, and sell it to you, I'd be a very rich man!

(18tonna88)

My father got me into supporting Celtic and now that he's gone, supporting them means more to me than ever. It ran in the family. My Dad's Granddad was instrumental in setting up the first supporters club in Lurgan (not the one that is there now.) It was, I think blown up. I see Celtic as much more than merely a football club. It is a way of life and a big family. Wherever you go in the world, seeing the hoops is an invitation to discuss all things Celtic with anyone. You will always have friends wherever you are, all because of a shared love of a football club. Supporting Celtic makes me proud when you think about the things we do. Bring Kano home, Thai Tims and all forms of charity. I live and breathe Celtic and they are always at the front of my thoughts. I can't imagine my life without Celtic. It would be, without a doubt, a much poorer existence.

(Morethanaclub)

Interview with Jay Beatty

Jay Beatty with the SPL trophy

Q) If you could go to any Celtic game, what game would you choose?

A) I just love Celtic so much and I don't care what game they are playing in. If I had the choice I would love them all to come to my house in Lurgan and play in my back garden against my friends. That would be the best game ever and I think Celtic would find it tough, though my Granda Hayden, who I would have in nets, has had both hips replaced so the defence would need to be strong for him. but I do love Cups and I would like to go to a cup final in Hampden and to win 3-2 with the third goal being scored in the last minute. I would go crazy and then I would go up with the team to collect the big trophy that would be a dream come true for me and to see all the fans singing and cheering us all on the lap of honour would be amazing.

Q) Only Celtic legends have songs written for them, so what is it like to have one written for you?

A) Wee Jay Celtic Bhoy is my favourite song and I cannot believe that Jim Scanlan has done a song for me, I just love it so much and am listening to it all the time. I hope people like it and will sing along to it and I just hope it makes people happy. I am only 11 and have only played once for Celtic and scored once so I am not really a legend but to have a Celtic song in your honour again shows that we are different from any other club and no matter what your ability is Celtic supporters will give you a chance. To everyone involved in the song I cannot thank you enough you have made me so proud and you have made my mummy cry with happiness every time she hears the song. To all the Celtic supporters, I love you all and if I ever get the chance to play for Celtic again and to score my daddy is bringing his step ladders with him to the game and I will get over that hoarding to celebrate and to give you all a hug.

Q) How does it feel to have scored a goal for Celtic?

A) As a football fan it is your dream to maybe one day play for your club, everyone has dreamt it at some stage in their lives but we all know that it only happens to a select few world class footballers. It is the only dream I had, every night before going to bed I was allowed to watch the clip of my hero samaras scoring against Rangers and diving into the crowd, it was my dream to someday be able to do this.

People may think that as I am an 11 year old wee 'Bhoy' with Down syndrome I would never get my wish but I always believed and supporting a club like Celtic you never know what might happen and in January 2015 my dreams came true. My heroes were playing away to Hamilton FC and I was allowed to give the team talk to Celtic in the changing room and then I was taken onto the pitch where I scored a cracking goal in front of a packed Stadium, I was just so happy and all the fans were going crazy, so I ran to them to celebrate and wanted to jump into their arms and hug them but could not get over the advertising hoarding as it was too big. But to hear all the fans singing my name around the stadium was the best day of my life and my mummy, daddy and Sister Olivia were so proud of me. My new dream is to watch Celtic win a cup final and to be allowed up with the captain to collect the trophy and to raise it above my head in front of all the Celtic fans. I BELIEVE!

Q) What is your favourite Celtic song?

A) Celtic songs are what make Celtic the best, we have had so many great songs over the years which supporters of other clubs instantly recognise. The Celtic song is a classic and I love hearing it, also the Willie Maley song up full blast in the car makes me so happy but my favourite song is 'Wee Jay Celtic Bhoy' which is a new song performed by Pat Scanlan and it's all about me. This is what makes us a special club, the fact that people would sit down write, produce and perform a song about me to raise money for our charity Down's & Proud. I love listening to my song and hearing others singing it makes me so proud.

Q) You give amazing team talks but if you had to tell a team why you love Celtic and why they are such a special club what would you say?

A) I would tell them that we are a club like no other, our history makes us special. We were founded in 1888 to help the Irish people who had nothing in Glasgow and we went from that to winning the biggest football trophy in Europe. Our strip of green and white hoops is like no other it is known throughout the world and as a support we never forget the legends that have pulled this jersey on. The fans have a passion like no other and to experience a packed Celtic Park under the flood lights on a European night is something that will change your life for ever. Celtic is NOT like other clubs we are unique and special. A club like no other.

Celtic means and represents a heartbeat.
(John O'Donnell)

Celtic is more than a club; it's a cause, a voice for the people. It's what can bind families together. Father son relationships, daughter and father, sister and brother, Mother and Father, it's what makes us as people. Going up to 'Paradise' every week on the bus, seeing the usual faces and being friendly and talking about the game the next day at school. When Celtic won against Barcelona I must have hugged at least ten strangers. It creates memories and moments we will never forget. That's what Celtic means to me.
(Rachel Docherty)

Celtic means passion to me.
(Cem Yildrim - Istanbul)

I've only started following Celtic recently but I've never experienced fans that are so united. Complete strangers openly talk to each other as if they are friends. They sing loud and proud all for one reason - the love of Celtic Football Club and what Celtic stands for. My only ever game was a pre-season match at Swansea, away. It was an atmosphere like no other I have experienced in my life; we lost but I can honestly say I've never had so much fun in all my life! Jumping and singing aloud for the full ninety minutes, we were constantly trying to drive the team forward. I don't care what anyone says about Celtic Football Club, they have the best morals and the best fans in the world by a long way! Celtic fans will back their club until the bitter end and will do whatever it takes to watch them be successful.
(Charlie Cheeseman)

There's nothing quite like walking through the gates of 'Paradise'. When I walk up the stairs and in to that fantastic arena, the hairs on my neck instantly stand so tall, just like the famous Glasgow Celtic. We have passion, a never give up attitude and pride; that's what we stand for.
(Thomas Mcgair)

I am a 52 year old protestant from Fife, now living in the midlands in England. I have been a Celtic supporter since I was five; I have never had any problems with the support. We represent inclusion.
(Gordon Murray)

Celtic Football Club is more than a Club, in some places it is a way of life and a community bond. The Club has wonderful charitable links and Irish heritage, making it very special. I think the thing that makes Celtic so unique is the atmosphere at the ground and the passion among the fans. I don't believe that any set of fans care about their team, quite as much as Celtic fans do, because as I have said previously: Celtic is a way of life and to some the Club is their life.
(Ciaran)

Everything about Celtic makes me proud. But you can't beat it when you are anywhere in the world and strangers that speak little English, shake your hand and say 'Celtic, good people'. You can't beat the pride you have when you hear that and people wanting your hoops top!
(Jimmy Mac)

From the States, Celtic means a familiarity and a sense of home, no matter where in the world you are. I've hugged people wearing the colours from Orlando to Oman, Seattle to Shanghai.
(Adam Chappelle)

Interview with Martin Smyth - owner of the 'Lennymobile'

Martin in his 'Lennymobile' car one St. Patrick's Day

Q) When did you first start travelling to Celtic matches & what is your abiding memory of those trips?

A) I have loved Celtic F.C. all my life but could never afford to travel to Scotland for matches.

Q) Have you been over to watch Celtic since moving to the USA and what is it like supporting Celtic from the States?

A) I moved to USA in 1997 when I was 25 years old. On January 19th 2000, I drove to Florida to watch Celtic F.C. play Tampa Bay Mutiny. It was my very first Celtic game. I met all the players and the manager as they were getting off the bus. Since then, I have travelled to Philadelphia, Connecticut, Washington DC, Toronto, Seattle & Chicago to watch Celtic play Man united, Liverpool Chelsea, Barcelona, etc.

I have met the players and socialised with them many times. Back home you wouldn't get too close to them, whereas in the USA I met them walking down the street. No one has a clue who they are! It would be like Donovan McNabb (Eagles) in Belfast, he could walk free, but not in Philly. In 2008 I met an American guy (Allan) in a Home Depot in Frazer PA, he was wearing a Celtic F.C. shirt. We got talking and traded phone numbers. A few days later we were talking on the phone, Phil O'Donnell had just died while playing for Motherwell, so we decided to go to Glasgow together for the weekend and catch the Charity Match they had for Phil's family. My wife was eight months pregnant with our first son (Eamon) at the time. Allan and I had both never been to Parkhead, so we acted on impulse and seized the opportunity. We stayed in a Hostel in Glasgow for two nights. We made some phone calls and talked to some people. After explaining our trip from USA, we gained access to the trophy room, the tunnel, the bench & were on the edge of the pitch at 'Paradise'. After the game we stayed in the car park and met Lenny and many others, including Wim Jansen.

Being a Celtic F.C. supporter in USA is so different, I spend all day explaining who & what Celtic F.C. The ONE thing that is unique about living in the USA is the fact that I have the freedom to support Celtic openly. Can you imagine me living in Scotland or Ireland with the 'Lennymobile' outside my house?

Q) What do you think that Celtic stands for and what does the Club mean to you?

A) Celtic is one of the biggest supported teams in the world and is known throughout the world for their passion and good behaviour. If you know your history, you will know we do not discriminate and all are welcome to play for or support our great club. Celtic is a club like no other. For as long as I can remember I have supported them and always collected shirts and memorabilia on my travels. I have had many hard times in my life, lost many things and also had many things taken from me. Nobody, I repeat nobody can take my love for Celtic away and trust me it is not something that can be lost either.

Q) How did the idea of the 'Lennymobile' start and could you tell us a little bit about your famous car?

A) I am a CNA (certified nursing assistant) and was working in a facility in Audubon PA in 2010. I drove a champagne coloured Buick LeSabre 1999. It was the best car that I had ever owned and I was not interested in any other car. An elderly lady, who was a patient asked my Co-worker Nicole, if Marty would be interested in buying her car. As it was a Buick, I was not interested. Nicole came back with more information. It was a 1999 Buick LeSabre, limited edition, had only one owner from new, had only 40,000 miles on the clock and was in mint condition. I bought it and gave my champagne Buick to my wife, scrapping her run around car. The only problem now was it was purple. I painted it 'Celtic green' and had a large Celtic sticker in my basement that I remember bragged it could stick to anything. It fitted perfect on the bonnet of my new car. I secured the edges of the sticker with green duct tape.

The reaction I was getting at traffic lights was crazy! Since then, I have added something every week to the 'Lennymobile'. I now have pictures taken daily. It brings a lot of joy into people's lives, just by driving it each day. I also have been in many parades and fund raising events with the 'Lennymobile'. On 'St. Patrick's Day' last year, my son and I were on the front page of the 'Philadelphia Daily News' in the 'Lennymobile' with a three page story inside. We were on 'Fox29'and 'Good Day Philadelphia' on St. Patrick's Day this year. All these things happened through meeting people in public that loved the car.

Q) Finally, of all your Celtic collection what is your favourite item in the car?

A) I have many priceless items but the most valuable item by far is a Celtic teddy bear that my mother gave to me when I was five years old. It has travelled all over the world with me. I gave it to my son, Eamon, on his fifth birthday and it is always in the back seat.

I was born into Celtic and wouldn't have it any other way. Friends and family may come and go but Celtic will always be there. It is that one love from birth until the moment you pass.
(Danie' Mcglade)

For me Celtic is a gift from God. You receive it the day you are born and it will never leave you. Anybody that receives this gift should thank their lucky stars!
(Kevin)

Father dear I oft times hear you speak of the Celtic team
You say they are the greatest club The world has ever seen.
You say the way they used to play they should get Champions belts
Now tell me Dad, the reason why you support the Celts.

My son, I've followed the Celtic team for 40 years or more,
I love to stand on Celtic Park and hear the faithful roar.
In Paradise, there always flies the flag of white and green
And that my son is the reason why I love the Celtic team.

In those bygone days the green jerseys were hated by all the DOBs
Oh how they dreaded to read about Shaw, McNair and Dodds
Who, for 15 weeks without a break, did keep their goal sheets clean
And that's another reason why I love my Celtic team.

Now there's no doubt that you'll read about 1938
When the Exhibition Trophy, that year it was at stake
Who beat the pride of England? the Bhoys in white and green
And that's another reason why I love my Celtic team.

Oh Father I will follow on wherever the Celts might go
I'll rise and fall by their football in spite of all their foe

I'll be the man to lead the van beneath the flag of green
And loud and high I'll raise the cry - God bless my Celtic
team.

That wee ditty and the John Thomson song was taught to
me by my Dad and by the time I was four I could sing
along with him. I started going to 'Paradise' when I was
seven, making the trip from Dalkey in Dublin. That was in
1956. Now I make the round trip from Coventry for every
home game. When I got home on Thursday morning after
Wednesday's game, my wife asked me if all was good. My
reply was, "It's great doing what I do in the place where I
belong - Celtic Park."
(Peter Dunne)

For me Celtic is the part of my life I look forward to every
single week. I was born into a Celtic family and brought up
with everything Celtic drummed into my head and for that
I'm glad. Celtic can be frustrating at the best of times but
when you're standing in a packed Celtic Park the feeling of
your hairs' standing up on the back of your neck and the
tingle down your spine when you see the players coming
out the tunnel makes it all worth it. I don't know what I
would do without Celtic as it's the biggest part of my life.
(Stephen Trainor)

To me Celtic means peace and quiet from the Mrs!
(Martin)

Interview with Darren O'Dea – former Celtic defender

Q) When you were playing for Celtic, did others in the team know about the history and culture of the Club?

A) I think most players when they sign for Celtic they see and think of the big Champions League nights and winning leagues and playing in Cup Finals. But the reality of Celtic is that it's more than just a football team. You represent a culture. You represent a massive history. If you haven't grown up in the Club or supported the Club then you can't understand it until you experience it so most players that come will learn as they go along. A lot of them take to it all great and love the admiration and love you get from Celtic fans. I would doubt they understand or know about the actual history but they will know and understand the passion and love the Club has. I always felt to play for Celtic and to be taken to by the fans; it wasn't just about playing well in a match. It was showing commitment to the Club and the cause. Whether that's taking time to sign autographs or acknowledge fans after long trips for away games. Obviously playing well was the main part but at a club like Celtic it's so much more. I do think that other players get that but only learn it as they go along.

Q) What do you think that the Celtic support stands for?

A) First and foremost it represents a fantastic football club. And supports the team everywhere it goes in the world. It's no coincidence everyone wants testimonials against Celtic as even 'friendlies' like this the fans will always turn out in incredible numbers. But Celtic is a way of life. The Club was set up with not football in mind but to help Irish immigrants. And I think that upbringing stems through the Club still to this day. The fact is Celtic is more than just a football team. It's a culture and way of life for people. It's a community! All be it a massive community. I've played in Canada, Ukraine and I've travelled to many countries in football and I always see people in Celtic jerseys. The Club has a worldwide community and even if you meet someone half way across the world who is a Celtic fan you immediately have a connection. It's one big Family.

Q) In your time as a player at the Club, which moment would you say was your favourite and which match had the best atmosphere?

A) I have so many fantastic memories of Celtic. Whether that's tommy burns flying me over as a 15 year old to try convince me to sign and he had Henrik Larsson come chat to me to talk about signing. Then making my debut against Inverness in the cup. Scoring my first goal against Dundee United. Playing in the last 16 in both legs against AC Milan. Winning the league at Kilmarnock when Naka scored that free kick. Scoring in the cup final against Rangers. I've loads more. But one always stands out and it might sound strange to other people but my best moment was making my Champions League debut against Copenhagen. I came on for the last thirty minutes and I think we lost 3-1. (It was 3-0 when I came on haha)... The reason this is my best moment is as a youth player the training we did was some of the hardest training I've ever done. Every day we'd work, work, work. We were a ridiculously fit team and technically very good as well.

Tommy burns worked us all as hard as I've ever seen. And the phrase he'd always tell us is "you're not training to be SPL players, your training to be Champions League players"... So all that graft and sweat and blood and tears became worth it when I made my champions league debut. I knew Tommy was proud as well of me, which when you made him proud you knew you were on the right road. So that always sticks with me.

The best atmosphere strangely enough I saw was against Man Utd in the Champions league when Naka scored 'that' free kick! I say it's strange because I didn't play and was on the bench. But sometimes when you're playing in games you are so focused that you don't take in everything, but that night was so special and the atmosphere was even more special.

Q) Finally, now that you have played for the Club and achieved success, what does Celtic mean to you?

A) Truthfully, Celtic means no more to me now than it did before my time or during my time there. I always knew about the history and culture and was always a fan. It's a club that just keeps moving along. I am lucky to be part of tiny bits of history with winning leagues and cups and that was always the aim when I started. Now I'm just part of a family. As a fan. But whether I was a player or now as a fan, I have always realised, understood and embraced what Celtic Football Club is. Hail Hail!

The Support's Special Moments

The Celtic support has always been special. It is likely that our unparalleled fan-base peaked in 2003 when the Club was estimated to have the backing of nine million people, including one million in the USA and Canada. Though it may be fair to assume that numbers have lowered since, there are still close to four hundred Celtic Supporters Clubs in over seventy countries worldwide; a seismic support by any reckoning.

The Celtic faithful have been described as "Famed for good behaviour, a valuable twelfth man." The most preeminent recognition of their nature was after the 2003 UEFA Cup Final. The Club's fans received awards from UEFA and FIFA for their exemplary conduct before, during and after the match. Upon presentation of the Fair Play Award, Celtic fans were hailed as "The greatest in the world."

The weight of support that Celtic carried to Seville (80,000 fans) for that UEFA Cup Final was not a one off. It is worth noting that the record Celtic Park attendance is 92,000, for a match versus Oldco Rangers in the league derby, on New Year's Day 1938. In fact, the Club holds the European record attendance, achieved at a home match, moved to Hampden Park in 1970, for the European Cup Semi Final v Leeds United. The crowd was officially announced as 136,505 but estimates of the genuine figure have been nearer to the 176,000 mark. However, the Scottish Cup Final of 1937, between Celtic and Aberdeen, holds the world record in all of club football: 147,365 the official attendance!

It should be stressed that attendances aren't the most imperative factor in the Celtic support though, rather the terrace culture and identity. The following moments indicate that Celtic fans can boast great distinction.

Glasgow's Green & White Exhibition:
In 1901, a tournament named 'The Glasgow International
Exhibition Cup' was won by Oldco Rangers. Glory was
achieved for the Govan Club when they defeated Celtic in
the final, held at Kelvingrove Park. Following the first
Ibrox disaster in 1902, the Huns put a competition on, with
the cup won the previous year offered as the prize. The
competition, named 'The British League Cup', was
honourably designed to raise funds for the families of the
disaster's victims. Celtic saw off Sunderland, whilst Oldco
Rangers beat Everton. It was all set for a Glasgow derby
finale. No quarter was given in a match drawn 1-1. Extra
time needed to be played and uncannily, the Hoops won 3-
2. Probably the incorrect etiquette, we then kept the trophy
for ourselves.

At the end of the season, Oldco Rangers directors' visited
Celtic Park to collect the trophy. However, feeling that we
had earned it, Celtic refused to hand it over! After legal
exchanges, which are rumoured to have continued into this
decade, the trophy remains at Celtic Park. It is still
engraved with the words: 'Won by Rangers FC.'

The moment links to the fans because of their hilarious
taunting over this in the 1910s and 1920s. For it was then
that Oldco Rangers sold their sporting soul and sought
success through sectarianism. It isn't an enormous feat, but
an interesting fact to begin with, before delving in to some
much more special moments.

Capital Comrades:
One of the earliest references to the Celtic support singing
at all comes from a 1911 encounter with Hibernian. The
instance in question stems from a report that fans of both
Clubs' shocked the establishment by singing 'God Save
Ireland' in unison! Almost two decades prior to that match,
T.D.Sullivan, MP and composer of the ballad; witnessed
his first Celtic game. He was feted by the Club, cheered by

the players and, in turn, sang a verse of his song. 'God Save Ireland', which remembers the Manchester martyrs, would prove an unofficial anthem for the support. Such is the importance of the song to Celtic's history, it had also been sung at the very meeting in which the idea of Celtic Football Club was instilled. The aforementioned moment from the match in 1911 merits its inclusion, simply because it is one of the first citations to Celtic supporters doing what they do best. Singing a song of such significance to boot!

We Are The Timalloys:
Celtic 5-1 Oldco Rangers, a Scottish Cup Semi Final played on 21st March 1925, before a then record 101,707 people. The match saw McGrory bag a hat-trick, a great moment in its own right. However, the scenes after the match are what were so remarkable. In the short time between the full time whistle and the start of celebrations, Celtic fans had quickly created a version of 'Hello Hello'.

Hello Hello we are the Timalloys
Hello Hello you'll know us by our noise
We beat the Rangers in the cup
Was great to be alive
Not one, not two, not three, not four but five!

The moment was brilliant and the song lasted a couple of years thereafter. It would return in a different guise, some years later.

They Come From Dear Old Donegal And Even From New York:
Tours of Europe had been taken by Celtic in 1904, 1906, 1907 and 1911. The Club was undeniably international at an early age and so the notion of travelling further afield, to undergo a tour of America, had already been contemplated in the early twentieth century. In 1910, Willie Maley travelled to New York with Celtic official, Tom Colgan.

The time was deemed inappropriate to take Celtic to the States as football wasn't established enough in the country. It wasn't until two decades later that a better time was viewed. In May 1931, the Celtic team, including Johnny Thompson and Jimmy McGrory boarded a boat from Yorkhill Quay. A great posse of fans gave the 'Bhoys' a warm Glasgow send-off but the greeting that waited across the pond was quite overwhelming.

Countless Scots and Irish had found a new life in America, some of whom were the wealthier Irish affected by the famine. They and their offspring had admired Celtic from afar. It was their sporting connection to home. When the Celtic team docked into the New York Bay after a gruesome journey, they were received by a congregation in frenzy. The sight of the Scottish Cup, paraded ashore, brought tears of joy and screams of felicity. The adulation was like that of a papal visit! Willie Maley recounted the disembarking of the ship: "Not once but on many occasions, I saw tears run down the cheeks of those who actually fought their way through the crowds to get a closer view of the cup."

The tour took in expatriate strongholds such as New York, Boston and Baltimore in the USA, before stretching to Toronto in Canada. Attendances surpassed ten thousand in nine of the thirteen matches. In the contests versus New York Giants and New York Hakaoh, held at the Polo Grounds, the attendances reached twenty thousand and thirty thousand respectively. That was the scale of Celtic. The prodigious 1931 tour was wholly memorable, the arrival scenes the most enduring image!

Forever In Our Hearts:
Though the bulk of these moments will be full of jubilation, there are some frankly extraordinary moments entwined with tragedy. Indeed, where there is sunshine, there must be shadow. That shadow fell on 9th September 1931 when

Johnny Thompson, 'The Prince of Goalkeepers', was laid to rest. Roughly forty thousand people attended his funeral in Cardenden, a considerable number of which had walked some fifty five miles from Glasgow. A further crowd about half the size turned out at Glasgow Queen Street station to watch two trains set off, carrying two thousand mourners. When you consider that the Club's average attendance never rose above eighteen thousand from 1930 until the suspension of football in 1938, the turnout to remember one of its most loved sons was nothing short of remarkable.

Johnny earned his status with his fantastic performances at such a young age. He was also a great character. A well-known quote, from when he was called a Fenian b*****d by an opposing player, is telling of his sense of humour. Johnny had reported the matter to his manager, James McGrory. McGrory replied: "Don't worry, I got called that all the time!" Thompson's retort: "Yes but you are one!" Johnny was of course a Protestant.

Johnny Thompson in action – late 1920s

We Rule Britannia:

At the opposite end of the decade, Celtic entered the
'Empire Exhibition Cup'. It was summer 1938 when
Glasgow hosted the event, in order to both boost the city's
economy and showcase the British Empire. A stunning
three hundred feet tall art deco tower was built on top of
Bellahouston Hill. This centrepiece of the Exhibition
dominated the city's skyline in all its magnificence. A
model of the tower was the prize on offer to the winning
football club. The best of British were invited to partake
but as irony would dictate, the club with an identity at polar
opposites to that of the Empire would win the competition.
At full time in the final (Celtic v Everton) hosted at Ibrox,
thousands upon thousands of Celtic fans broke into a
rousing chorus of 'The Dear Little Shamrock.' The fan's
favourite ballad being sang with such gusto marked the
occasion powerfully!

The Flag That Flies On High:

Again involving a ballad, this time in 1952, the Celtic fans
sang a less common song for the football: 'Kevin Barry'.
Thought to be penned by a Glasgow Irish immigrant in the
1920s, the Celtic support would have been familiar with the
lyrics, which had a rather anti-British sentiment in the
original version. It was just five days sooner, on February
11th, that the Club had received instruction from the SFA to
remove the Irish tri-colour from the stadium. The body had
held an investigation into the violence at an earlier Celtic v
Oldco Rangers match, which concluded that the flag should
be taken down as it had been to blame for inciting the
trouble.

The national flag of Ireland was and still is an essential
symbol of the Club and its heritage. The particular flag
flown above the Jungle at the time had been handed to

Celtic Football Club by Eamon De Valera (then Irish Prime Minister). It was a gift that would not be readily removed.

You may just be able to spot the Irish tri-colour on the flag pole between the floodlight pylon and the Jungle stand. (Janefield Cemetery is behind and the Celtic End is to the left as we look.) – Old Celtic Park image donated from Jamie Fox's collection.

At this period, Celtic was in fact third from bottom in the league table. Yet a crowd of more than twenty thousand had turned up to watch them brush aside Stirling Albion. The sense of discontent was palpable: "Another martyr for old Ireland, another murder for the crown, whose brutal laws may kill the Irish, but can't keep their spirits down," rang out from pockets of the Celtic support queuing to gain entry to the ground. Newspapers of the time likely extenuate the number of those singing, but given that doing so wasn't a widespread terrace activity back then, the moment must have been special all the same.

Chairman, Robert Kelly, famously claimed that he would "Rather remove Celtic from Scottish football and start playing Gaelic games at Celtic Park," than to comply with the order. Eventually, Scottish clubs had a vote on the matter. Many (including Hibernian) voted against the flag being flown and it all came down to the decision of Oldco Rangers. The self-proclaimed 'quintessential British Club' decided that the flag of Ireland should be permitted to ripple in the wind above Celtic Park. That fact isn't as ironic as it may seem. For in order for the dead Club to succeed, they needed that emblem of Irishness across the city: a representation of the very thing they had become the antithesis of.

King John Bonnar:

A year later, Celtic found themselves on the crest of a wave. The dark post war years appeared to have been overcome and the flag controversy was resolved. Wider society too, experienced change. Queen Elizabeth II took to the throne and as such, football commemorated the occasion by holding an inaugural competition. Held in Glasgow, four teams from England and Scotland were invited to take part in the 'Coronation Cup'. Celtic was only handed an invitation because of their ability to attract large crowds.

Amazingly, the Hoops reached the final of the competition at Hampden Park. There they met Hibernian. A green and white crowd of 117,060 paid witness to a Celtic victory by two goals to nil. Celtic owed their triumph to keeper John Bonnar, whom the Club had tried to rid themselves of just months earlier. His outstanding display had made all the difference and a string of saves meant that masses of Hoops fans gathered at the front entrance of the stadium to congratulate him. Songs and smiles filled the lengthily wait for the hero of the hour. Eventually, fans jumped, pointed and then yelled his name repeatedly as he emerged. The sheer exuberance was unbelievable. Celtic had again won a competition celebrating British imperialism, despite being totally opposed to it!

It's Enough To Make Your Heart Grow...:
Fourteen years later, Celtic were again on the cusp of glory. By hook, crook, bus, plane, train and automobile; thousands of supporters had made it to Lisbon for the final of the 1967 European Cup. The faithful had won the hearts of the Portuguese with their exemplary conduct and admirable atmosphere before the match. No moment did they do so more, than immediately before kick-off. As the Celtic players lined up alongside their Italian opponents in the tunnel, Bertie Auld cleared his throat and began to sing: "Sure it's a grand old team to play for..." Each of the Lisbon Lions joined in and Glen Daly's immortal Celtic anthem soon became detectable to the supporters. In perhaps the most beautiful moment of Celtic's history, the support sang it too, as the players came in to view. "Sure it's a grand old team to see and if you know your history..." The players and fans enjoying the occasion appeared to mesmerise the Inter Milan outfit and already Celtic had the upper hand. The moment has to be regaled as one of the best in the Club's history!

Of course the outcome of the match in Lisbon created greater history in its own right. The result sparked wild scenes and adding to the mayhem was a certain Charles Patrick Tully! How fitting it was that the man who had such influence over 'The Celtic Song' should experience the moment at first hand. It is well documented that Belfast Celtic, Tully's home Club, used to sing 'Darn the hare we care, because we only know that there's going to be a show and the Belfast Celtic will be there.' On a visit to London to record 'The Celtic Song', Glen Daly found himself without a completed second verse but with an hour until he was due in the studio! He remembered the words that Charlie Tully had sang to him one evening in Kenilworth and scribed the lyrics. The anthem was complete.

Glen Daly's iconic melody would have almost certainly been roared at Celtic Park the day following the Lisbon miracle as well. Hundreds of thousands of supporters back in Glasgow had gathered in the ground and on surrounding streets to welcome the Lisbon Lions home. The Lions, symptomatic of their modesty as local working class men, were parading the European Cup on the back of a coal lorry! After they had done their laps around the track surrounding the pitch, the terraces emptied. People were spreading themselves across the hallowed turf and putting chunks of the playing surface into their pockets as souvenirs. The buzz about the city was outrageous – another superb scene from a golden period in our history.

The crowds gather to see the European Cup at Celtic Park

A closer look at the Lisbon Lions with the European Cup –
Image donated from Jamie Fox's collection

Oh The Celtic Supporters Were Shouting That Day:
From the heat of Portugal to the cool of England, again in
the centre of European success; Celtic were bound for
Yorkshire. It was there that a team dubbed 'England's
greatest' lay in wait. Just six thousand tickets were made
available to the Celtic faithful but an estimated thirteen
thousands fans travelled down. The demand was so great
that British Rail put on a 'Football Special' service. The
train departed Glasgow soon after midday and arrived in
Leeds some five hours later. 'The Yorkshire Post' said of
the support: "Nothing has happened quite like it in
Yorkshire since the Roman legions left York."

The trip to Leeds was unique. On the journey down, the
Celtic squad were entertained by Ranger's fanatic and great
comedian Lex McLean. Then Celtic were required to wear
alternative coloured socks to avoid a kit clash. Of the red or
blue socks available, Jock Stein elected for his side to don
the red pair. He claimed that: "The socks will look orange
under the lights. It'll look like we are wearing the colours
of the tri-colour, that'll please the fans." The result itself
was also unique in that it was the first victory on the road
throughout the season's European campaign.

With that said, the moment of focus is on the 'Football
Special'. The trip made for an atmospheric and drink
fuelled journey and as the conclusion neared, the singing
escalated. Carriages holding hundreds were swaying to the
sounds of familiar old cries of rebellion. Mixed in were
tales of Celtic's great history and foregone legends. With
the station in sight a great cheer went up and voices arose
from the rear of the carriage: "Said Lizzie to Phillip as they
sat down to dine, I've just had a note from an old friend of
mine." The rest of the train clapped, stamped and thudded
the roof to the beat. A sense of community and passion
rang true. The version continued with great resonance,
hitting a crescendo with the lyrics: "To keep Celtic down
you will have to deport the fighting mad Irish/whole Fenian

army that gives them support!" The moment was loud but magical.

England Sent Their Very Best And They Didn't Meet With Much Success:

The return leg of the European Cup tie against Leeds was interpolated with raucous noise. Celtic had earned a hard fought victory at Elland Road two weeks previous and needed to see off any fight back to book a place in the European Cup Final for a second time. The game was played at Hampden on 15th April 1970. It would be played in front of a European record 136,505 people (4,000 Leeds fans). Just shy of the fifteen minute mark, the masses were briefly silenced when Billy Bremner struck a belter right into the stanchion. The tie was level. Then probably the single loudest and most intense chant in our history started. "Celtic! Celtic! Celtic! Celtic!" It seeped round the ground, gaining speed and boisterousness. Soon the 132,000 plus Celtic contingent were belting the Club's name as one. You can only imagine the noise that the sound of so many people screaming in defiance would have generated. Billy Bremner alludes to the moment in an interview when he says: "I'd told the boys, `Don't be intimidated by the crowd,' but I knew we had to quiet them early on. Then it started: 'Celtic, Celtic.' It is a noise like that which made many an Englishman freeze in internationals!"

Win, Lose Or Draw:

Celtic defeated Leeds to advance to their second European final. Off the park, the supporters too had made their mark. The Celtic contingent was praised by the media either side of the border for their behaviour, humour and great turnouts at both matches. This vain continued at the final in Milan, where Feyenoord provided the ultimately superior competition. Despite the football downfall, the Celtic faithful showed their sportsmanship once more. The occasion was in contrast to Lisbon, three years its former. The weather was dull and dreary and the Celtic team played poorly. Feyenoord deservedly won the cup with a 2-1 victory after extra time. It was a touching moment at full time though, when the majority of the twenty thousand Celtic fans gave their Dutch counterparts a rapturous applause and standing ovation. Our magnanimous reaction to defeat seemed to touch many connected with the Rotterdam Club. The gesture is well summarised by Feyenoord's goalkeeper of the time, Eddy Pieters: "It will stick in my mind forever that the Celtic players and fans all stayed and gave us a round of applause as we lifted the cup."

Softly Sung Celts:
Mid-way through the seventies, the most successful years of the Club were ending. Times were by no means tough but they were changing. One of the big changes on the terraces was when 'You'll Never Walk Alone' was replaced for a brief period. Hearing thousands of Celtic fans, scarfs aloft in 'walk on' fashion – it was one of Rod Stewart's most enjoyable moments as a Celtic fan. No doubt you have deduced that the replacement song was a Rod Stewart single: a number one in September 1975 at that. Rod is a well-known Celtic fan and he had enjoyed some sustained success on the pop music scene in the seventies. During the 1975/1976 season, as the teams took to the field, the Jungle decided to deviate from tradition. The occupants raised their scarfs as usual but the lyrics weren't in keeping with the norm. "We are sailing, we are sailing, home again, across the sea, we are sailing, stormy waters, to be near you, to be free," oozed from Glaswegian lips. It caught on well but despite its beauty, the song was short lived. The fans returned to 'You'll Never Walk Alone' soon after. Nonetheless, that first rendition was a fine moment and certainly enhanced by the element of surprise.

Fewer By One But Defeated The Hun:
The seventies ended in a typical manner. Yet again Celtic
Football Club was involved in one of the biggest matches
in Scottish football history. The match in question brought
the curtain down on the 1978/1979 season for Celtic. It was
May 21st and Celtic Park staged a title decider against
Oldco Rangers. Only a win would suffice for the Hoops but
Oldco Rangers could afford the luxury of a draw; with a
further game to play. A ferociously partisan crowd was
audible long before kick-off but fell eerily quiet in the
opening exchanges. Perhaps that was a testament to the
nerves felt by both supports. Alex MacDonald gave Oldco
Rangers the lead inside ten minutes and placed the 'Bhoys'
in real trouble. Then disaster struck, early in the second
half, when Johnny Doyle was given his marching orders for
violent conduct! His dismissal all but signified the end for
Celtic.

The Celtic fans refused to accept defeat, especially not with
the league trophy leaning towards Ibrox. A battle like cry
sounded out around the stadium. Every Celtic voice box
became active if not broken. 'Paradise' was bouncing. The
atmosphere culminated in a particularly hair standing
rendition of the Celtic version of 'Hail Glorious Saint
Patrick': "In the war against the Rangers in the fight for the
cup, Jimmy McGrory put the Celtic one up, we've done it
before and we'll do it again, on Erin's green valley's look
down on Parkhead!" People normally unanimated, even in
the seated stand, appeared to join in with fervour. It was
awe inspiring.

Buoyed by such vociferous support, Celtic secured the title
in the game's dying embers. "Ten men won the league tra-
la-la-la-la," ricocheted off the walls of Celtic Park. The
reaction to Doyle's ordering off was something that should
always be remembered. The night was iconic in
atmosphere.

The Love (Street) Of Stealing Titles:
The eighties proved an exciting era for Scottish football fans. Aberdeen, Hearts, Dundee United, Oldco Rangers and Celtic all achieved considerable feats at different times. But perhaps Dundee and a certain Albert Kidd will be most fondly remembered by the Celtic support, when thinking of the era. Of course that is because of the role they/he played in the astonishing twist of the title in 1986. May the third, Celtic played at Love Street against a St. Mirren side of reasonable quality. Concurrently, Hearts visited Dundee at Dens Park. The situation was simple. To become champions, Celtic had to win by three goals and hope that Hearts suffered defeat.

Both games entered the final ten minutes: St Mirren 0-5 Celtic, Dundee 0-0 Hearts. The sense of inevitability dampened the mood. Though, the Celtic support gathered around anybody with a Walkman Radio and focused on the proceedings at Dens.

On the Love Street pitch before the fans, Paul McStay broke down the right wing and looped a cross into the keeper's arms. "YASSSSSSSSSSSSSSSSSSS!!!!" The mood was brightened like a blazing sunrise. News had filtered through that Albert Kidd had given Dundee the lead! "YASSS!!" "YASSSSS!!!" There was elation around Love Street. People were leaping up one step and ending five below! The goalkeeper held the ball and froze, a look of perplexion entrenched across his face. Of all conquests in the history of Celtic Football Club, that was certainly the most unexpected.

Scenes after full time at Love Street

Faithful Through And Through:

In defence of the 1985/1986 title, Celtic lost out to Oldco Rangers by six points. The bid to reclaim champion status was underway and on Saturday 12th December 1987, Celtic entertained again title contenders, Heart of Midlothian. Coincidentally, the day brought recurrently fabulous scenes at the Jambo's expense. Hearts had gotten themselves two goals ahead with that cursed closing ten minute period to see out. Uncannily, Andy Walker popped up with a fine finish to halve the deficit. The superb support for Celtic was then almost sucking the ball into the net for an equaliser. In the fan's endeavour, a special moment transpired in the eighty fifth minute when the Celtic End started a particular rallying cry: "We are Celtic supporters faithful through and through." The Jungle joined and started to sway in its unique way. An equaliser seemed imminent. "Over and over we will follow you!" The rising volume ushered the team forward, soon paying dividends as Paul McStay smashed in an absolute screamer from just outside the box. Celtic had stolen a point. McStay sprinted along the touchline and dived in to the Jungle. Cue a carbon copy of Love Street style celebrations!

Come On Over To My Place:

If anything, the eighties exemplified the character of the Celtic support to produce something special in adverse times. The centenary season was one of huge success, but it also showed that defiance isn't always a result of difficulty. No occasion was this displayed more so than on a dark Wednesday evening, March 30th 1988. Celtic had recorded a victory by a goal to nil at Pittodrie. In sinking Aberdeen, the Hoops had not only extended their unbeaten run to twenty eight matches, but they had also all but sealed the title. This gave the five thousand travelling support something to celebrate. As one might expect, the celebrations went long in to the night. Surprisingly, those celebrations took place inside Pittodrie. 'We Shall Not Be Moved' and 'Happy Birthday Dear Celtic' were sung with buoyancy, among others. To rid the stadium of the exhilarated away support, the floodlights were switched off. It is at that point that the ability to show defiance, in joy, was reinforced. 'We're Not Going Anywhere' was the chant of the Celtic fans, coupled with the ignition of lighters. The party in the lit up sky went on and on and was the beginning of a great continuous celebration all the way to the Scottish Cup Final.

Happy Birthday Celtic:
The archetypal scene of the decade undoubtedly arrived in May 1988. Indeed there can be no match that is more illustrative of the Celtic support than the 1988 Scottish Cup Final. Before kick-off, both Dundee United and Celtic fans held up a red card display to Margaret Thatcher, who had been invited to present the trophy. The match itself typically saw two late McAvennie goals clinch glory. But my particular focus is the post-match jubilation, simultaneous with Tommy Burn's famous interview.

After full time there were an astronomical number of tri-colours flying from all quarters of an overflowing Hampden Park. Tens of thousands of green and white shirts, scarfs and flags provided fabulous colour. The noise was electric. History had been created and celebrated. Frankly, a picture paints a thousand words, but before doing so, the comments of a Tommy Burns moved to tears, come as close as it gets to a suitable description: "That's what's so special about them right there. Just right up there, that's what's so special about them. They're there and they're always there. And God bless every one of them."

Picture overleaf:

Celtic fans sing YNWA as they sense victory at the Centenary Cup Final

Don't Be Afraid Of The Dark:

Little shy of a year beyond our centenary, the support caught the attention for different reasons. The actions of the Club and fans alike could not bestow a greater epitome to what makes following Celtic so special; than during the benefit match organised at Parkhead to help raise funds for the families affected by the Hillsborough disaster. The match saw a crowd of over sixty thousand take to the terraces.

Prior to kick off, without being manufactured by lead singers or stereo systems, the Jungle punters raised their scarfs. Fittingly, they sang like they so often do: "When you walk through a storm." Side by side, both sets of supporters gave a sincere airing of their shared anthem, in tribute to the ninety six supporters who went to a football match and never came home. The moment was loud, genuine lump in the throat material and a real exhibition of the charitable ethos of the Club.

Billy Bhoys:

I feel it all to appropriate to climb into the painful decade that was the nineties, with the theme of us getting one over our former rivals. I cast back to the half time interval on 17th March 1991. Celtic were down to ten men but two goals to the good, in a game that eventually saw three Oldco Ranger's players ordered off. During the said interval, a new song of mockery was heard for the first time. The Celtic bellow was to the tune of a normally harrowing song: "HAHA, HAHA, HAHAHAHAHAHA, HAHA, HAHA, HAHAHAHAHAHA," it went. Not only were the Celtic faithful satirising the Oldco Rangers' form of support, but doing so to the tune of 'The Billy Boys!'

The match was won 2-0 and the game is still famously revered as the 'Saint Patrick's Day Massacre.' The half time chant of tumultuous laughter lived until the death of our neighbours and always served as a favourite source of infuriation. The teasing song was a fabulous invention, simply for its ability to contrast our humour with the Hun's lack of it.

Let The People Sing:

Of course a vital facet in the uniqueness of our support is our musical culture. No doubt the Scottish and Irish musical influence has led to some of the finest songs in football being written for the Club. Therefore, it should come as no surprise that fine moments and Folk music have been interlinked at some stage in Celtic's history.

The moment elected is the opening of 'The Blarney Pilgrim's' performance in McNees, Glasgow, on St Patrick's night 1991. Punters arrived in good spirits, especially given that the affectionately termed 'Saint Patrick's Day Massacre' (earning its name through the victory against Oldco Rangers amongst a host of red cards) had taken place earlier in the day.

A soft whistle of a flute and gentle strum of a guitar signified the start of the gig. The lyrics to 'Foggy Dew' accompanied the music, poured from the heart of the lead singer and among the consuming audience. Strong passion and the sense of being part of a unique culture carried the set forward in enthralling fashion.

'The Blarney Pilgrims' band has been an instrumental part of the Glasgow Irish music scene, quite literally, and the strength that the circuit currently enjoys in Scotland is largely down to them. Sadly, members Mick and James left the band later in the decade to form 'Athenrye'. As a duo, they had great success and toured with 'The Wolfe Tones' at one stage. Thankfully this gig was recorded though and can be found on YouTube to this day. Many a fan has expressed that McNees, in the 1990s, with 'The Pilgrims', were the greatest times. Having heard the recording, I concur!

Our Stories And Our Songs:
In further celebration of the story of Celtic, tangibly connected to the famine, 'The Fields of Athenry' hit the terraces in 1994. The world famous Irish ballad became a regular song heard among the Celtic support, after it was sung away at Ibrox that year. The ballad was a familiar song in the Irish communities worldwide but hadn't been sung as a 'Celtic choir' at the time. Elegant and emotive, the away support began to sing: "By a lonely prison wall, I heard a young girl call-all-all-ing…"

The fact that the song was instigated against Oldco Rangers prompted allegations of sectarianism at the time. Accusations were allayed with the claim that Celtic had used the ballad to incite a response from the Oldco Rangers support. That assertion was wide of the mark because the song tells the tale of hardships during the famine, a historical event that is inextricably linked to the Irish emigrates in Scotland and subsequent founding of Celtic

Football Club. Therefore, in April 1996, writer, Pete St. John was invited to Celtic Park to emblazon his ballad on the Celtic support. At half time of a match against Falkirk, Pete took to the field and began to sing. He was not alone as the stands reprised the lyrics: "Low lie the fields of Athenry, where once we watched the small free birds fly (Hey baby let the free birds fly), our love was on the wing, we had dreams and songs to sing, it's so lonely around the fields of Athenry."

I felt compelled to include the scene because of its emotion and uniqueness. It is simply unimaginable to think that any other club would sing such a song and for something of its ilk to be appropriate at a football game outside of ourselves.

Broken Radio, Broken Aberdeen:
Breaking from the chronology, I turn the clock back ever so slightly to April 1st of 1996. The Hoops played host to Aberdeen in a half complete Celtic Park, which was undergoing renovation. By the second half, Celtic were oozing panache. Striking sensation, Jorge Cadete, then finally made his debut in the game as a substitute. No sooner did he enter the field of play than join the party with a cracking goal. The strike was met with an almighty roar that genuinely blew 'BBC Radio Scotland' and 'Radio Five Live' off air! A combination of the quality on show and the eagerly awaited arrival of Cadete produced such a response.

Cadete of course, had been itching to get a taste of the action for some six weeks since being introduced to the crowd at a home match v Partick Thistle. Neither he nor Celtic could have anticipated an 'issue' with the paperwork over his registration. It later transpired that the delay had been deliberately manufactured by Jim Farry, Chief Executive of the SFA. Farry's partiality against Celtic had ensured that the elite striker missed out on a number of matches, which likely cost Celtic the title. His position became untenable and his P45 was quite rightly handed to him as a result.

The registration problem wasn't the only time that Jorge Cadete would experience controversy in Scotland. In the following campaign, aimed at stopping 'the nine', he netted a fantastic volley to pull Celtic level in the 'New Year's Derby'. Only to find that as he wheeled away, the linesman had raised his flag for offside – a disgraceful decision and pure act of cheating. The decision denied Celtic a point. Losing three points to our competitors, as opposed to sharing the spoils, was a critical moment in quelling our title challenge.

Cheerio To Ten In A Row:
The nineties had been a very painful decade for everybody connected to Celtic. However, 1998 produced one of the absolute finest achievements in the history of the Club. Of course I am talking about the day we 'stopped the ten'. I feel it impossible not to relive the celebrations on the Gallowgate that day. After the sensational atmosphere, subsequent pitch invasion and trophy presentation; it seemed every Celtic fan in the city adjourned to the area. Cars and supporters buses were piled back up the road in huge traffic, thanks to the sporadic huddles breaking out and spilling all along the street. Horns were beeping and tooting in delight, buses bouncing, huge flags waving and grown men crying. It was carnage. After so much hurt, so much mockery, Celtic finally brought down Oldco Rangers. There is perhaps no club in the world that can experience that level of emotion, a typical Celtic moment and for many, the greatest day of their lives.

Celtic Get The Place Rocking:
Two years later and in a far less important match, the Hoops support created an unusual yet equally raucous moment. Celtic fans had travelled to Anfield in great

numbers to see their team participate in Ronnie Moran's Testimonial. With an hour to go until kick off, the stands began to fill and the Celtic end was literally jumping. Remarkably, the stadium genuinely wobbled! Liverpool had to reduce the capacity of the stand after the match until further construction be carried out. Speaking of the matter, a spokesman for Liverpool City Council said: "People were jumping up and down on a repeated basis and shouting and it affected the stand's dynamic loading. It was very unusual and different to a normal football crowd."

Twelve Yard Twirl:
Beyond the turn of the millennium, Celtic played Champions League finalists of the foregone season, Valencia. The tie went to penalties. Paul Lambert stepped up first and put Celtic into the lead in the shootout. As the poor Valencia player left the half way line to take his penalty, there was a deafening hail of boos and hisses to put him off. As he addressed the ball, the entire support twirled their scarfs, which whipped across his line of vision. He coolly slotted home and the ground fell silent. The pattern was repeated for each Valencia player to take a spot kick. The intensity of the booing and scarf waving became greater each time and reached a crescendo for the spot kick taker that followed Henrik Larsson's dire miss. Sadly it proved fruitless as Valencia won on sudden death.

Though defeated, the spectacle was unforgettable. The sight of those scarfs being twirled and the intimidating noise that the support created was simply superb. The whole night was mesmeric because of the height of atmosphere that had been created. Martin O'Neill often spoke of the evening as the 'benchmark for European football.' Typical Celtic.

Come Fly With Me:
Painstaking as losing out to Valencia was: the foundations for special European nights under Martin O'Neil had been

laid. As every Celtic fan knows, we made it all the way to the UEFA Cup Final in 2003. Some fabulous outfits were eliminated along the way and we played some smashing football. The Celtic squad's emergence at Oporto airport, having snatched victory against Boavista in the Semi Final, ranks as high as any moment in the run. Celtic Football Club was the words on the lips of journalists throughout the UK and images of the scene were beamed throughout the country.

Celtic supporters were flying home, Porto fans were arriving and both were in ecstatic mood. There was a good natured sing off when suddenly Celtic fans went absolutely crazy. The team had arrived ready to fly back to Glasgow and they were completely mobbed by the adoring support. An image that stands out is of Stylian Petrov ending in the centre of the crowd and Henrik Larsson stood behind him with a green and white scarf draped over his shoulder. The best summarisations are again the comments of Martin O'Neill: "I doubt if I will ever forget the scenes at Oporto airport after the Boavista game. The fans spend a lot of money to come and cheer us on, behave impeccably, and I can assure you it is appreciated in the dressing room!"

Beach Ball Sunday:
Sandwiched between the Oporto airport scene and the UEFA Cup Final was 'Beach Ball Sunday!' Celtic found their opponents in the shape of Oldco Rangers at Ibrox. The race for the title was still very much on.

Outside Ibrox that day, two Celtic fans sat in deck chairs wearing Hawaiian shirts. Once in the ground, the great banter and wit of the Celtic hoarders was shown. Beach ball after balloon and lilo after rubber ring inadvertently made their way onto the playing surface. The match referee was left with no option but to delay kick off by some twenty minutes. Who could forget that vista of inflatables?

The banter refused to draw to a close, even after a clear playing surface was restored. The full Celtic end belted "No Huns in Europe, oh there'll be no Huns in Europe," following kick off. A final farewell was offered before the full time whistle as Celtic expressed their wit continentally: "Adios, Adios, Adios," replaced traditional chants of 'cheerio'. It was a great display of sportsmanship and good natured patter.

Inflatables at Ibrox – Images donated from Jamie Fox's collection

Seville And The King Of Kings:
Reaching the last stage in a European competition was a
phenomenal achievement for Celtic, and the support that
the 'Tims' had given the team along the way, even better.
The good natured invasion of the lovely Spanish city was
riddled with moments to remember. Perhaps the greatest
moment of the trip was when Henrik Larsson scored his
second stunning header of the match, to bring the score line
back to level pegging. As the 'King of Kings' rose to meet
Alan Thompson's delivery and guide the ball to its rightful
destination, a crazy roar of brobdingnagian proportions was
released. The stadium nigh on exploded. The majority of
Celts watching on the big screen in the city centre were
bouncing in the manner of salmon. Every Celtic minded
man, woman and child beamed like nothing that a laser has
ever been capable.

"You are my Larsson, my Henrik Larsson, you make me
happy when skies are grey, we went for Shearer, but he's a
w****r, so please don't take my Larsson away." The
euphoria bounded across the city square. Almost
concurrently, those fortuitous to be inside the stadium
screamed the same. It was without doubt the most
atmospheric moment that any city would have experienced
in football.

Celtic fans walk the streets of Seville in their masses

Madrid Shall Never Walk Alone:
This chosen moment is from a European night again but it demonstrates another way in which the support gets its magnetism. The first of a two legged affair in the 2004 UEFA Cup last sixteen was given greater import because of a tragic bomb blast in Madrid, during the build-up to the game. The Celtic family offered real compassion to their Spanish counterparts.

In a way that only Celtic fans are capable, we responded with an emotional rendition of 'You'll Never Walk Alone'. The stadium announcer informed the crowd that the traditional pre match anthem would be sung in tribute to those affected in the Spanish capital. In conjunction with his announcement, the teams emerged from the dressing rooms to a lethal roar of approval. The Parkhead stereo system aired the piercing words 'When you walk through a storm.' Then as one, the fans each raised their scarfs and flags. This was singular. A truly poignant moment, symptomatic of what the Celtic support is all about. There were Swedish flags, Catalonian flags and a vast array of green and white scarfs. Everybody had something to show.

The lyrics reached 'walk on' when as usual the recording was stopped to allow the Celtic fans to take over. Takeover they did! The volume cranked to heights seldom heard before. "Through the wind, walk on through the rain…" each quadrant of the stadium continued.

The players had taken to their positions on the field by that point. This allowed the television camera to momentarily pan round to the Celtic dugout. In view were David Marshall and Martin O'Neill. Both stood gazing around the stadium in utter disbelief at what they were witnessing. That scene, shown around the footballing world, encapsulates exactly why the Celtic fans are so different to any other. As the song concluded, the commentary team broke their silence with words that reverberate the moment:

"It may be a bitterly cold evening here at Celtic Park but nothing can disguise the genuine emotion, as the Celtic supporters in their own unique way, pay tribute and offer condolences in song."

Something Inside So Strong:
Forward to the current decade, I have decided to relive some moments from the 2010/2011 season, combining them into a collective piece. In a season when Celtic had to endure bigotry, violence and corruption; there arose the strongest sense of unity for many a year.

The season had seen penalty awards being overturned and officials lying to cover up the process behind the removal of the spot kick. Thanks to the resignation of one official, who exposed the cover up, a host of further SFA resignations were to follow. That initial bonding through injustice grew greater when Neil Lennon received an extensive ban for his part in an altercation with Oldco Rangers' Assistant Manager, Ally McCoist. Among the commotion of an evening whereby Oldco Rangers had three players sent off, their players had manhandled the referee, El Hadji Diouf had elbowed the Celtic physiotherapist and Ally McCoist had provoked Neil Lennon with a yet to be revealed comment; only Lennon received a ban.

However, a greater unifying force was in motion. It was bigotry and it was coming from all over Scotland. The hate campaign was aimed at our leader, the unashamed Lurgan Catholic, Neil Lennon.

In April 2011, Celtic made the short journey to Kilmarnock. In the lead up to the game, Neil Lennon, QC Paul McBride and MP Trish Goodman (all prominent Celtic fans) had been the target of bigoted thugs, who had attempted to send them nail bombs. A lovely moment transpired in the eighteenth minute of the match when the

Celtic fans at either end of the ground broke into applause for two minutes. Eighteen was Lennon's squad number as a player with the Club and the applause was an act of support for him.

Despite the protests of the Celtic faithful, the sectarian hate refused to conclude. Barely five minutes into the second half of an infamous night in the capital, Celtic had taken a two goal lead against Hearts. Naturally, Neil Lennon was delighted, but his delight was short lived. A Hearts fan made way for the dugout and attacked him at pitch side. The incident was shameful, as were the cheers of approval by the Heart's fans. They serenaded the Celtic support with a distasteful rendition of their version of 'The Billy Boys'. The mention of being "Up to their knees in Fenian blood," proved too much for the Celtic supporters and they set about drowning out the home fans. The full travelling support bounced up and down, arms aloft and as loud as possible, they returned the favour: only we showed a little more class than our sectarian counterparts. An unambiguous "When I see you Celtic, I go out of my head, I just can't get enough," was directed at the opposing support. Jaws had dropped and the home contingent fell silent. The sight of the full stand jumping was sensational. (The attacker was found not guilty. The evidence seen live on Sky Sports was not sufficient for a conviction.)

The 2010/2011 campaign did also provide some relief and the platform for the first mass huddle. On February 20th, as Celtic held a healthy lead over Oldco Rangers, the Green Brigade decided to milk the moment. On this occasion, the rest of Celtic Park wanted a piece of the action. Not dissimilar to a Mexican wave, section after section gradually became involved until the foundations of 'Paradise' were rocking under the weight of sixty thousand leaping Celts.

The huddle at Celtic Park – Image courtesy of
Vagelis Georgariou

The last game before the curtain came down on the season
saw Celtic break from the tradition of the team walking out
to 'The Celtic Song'. Instead the PA system serenaded Neil
Lennon with a rendering of 'Something inside so strong'.
Then as the news spread that the title would almost
certainly be in Oldco Ranger's hands, Celtic fans found a
loud voice from deep within their hearts. They regaled tales
of their heroes in song. Henrik Larsson. Tommy Burns.
Jimmy Johnstone. It was a wonderful show of faith.

Banner for Neil Lennon – Image courtesy Green Brigade

Fifteen Minutes Of Fun:

A season later, the Celtic support was creating new memorable occasions. At half time in football matches, especially in the modern game, fans can sit down and take a rest or tuck into overpriced refreshments if they wish. The Celtic contingent at Inverness decided to put on a show instead. The interval was well documented and has since become known as 'the greatest half time show ever.'

It was February 2012 and the game at the Caledonian Stadium was a bit dull. A few reports before the match had started to become a little more sincere regarding Oldco Rangers and their financial turmoil. So the Celtic away fans decided to celebrate the demise of their foes. Hundreds of people gathered on the concourse and began doing the conga and huddle, each "When Rangers die." The longest chant soon sprung up: "The Huns are going bust...AGAIN!" Throughout the break, the fans didn't stop screaming that cry. What a fabulous break in play.

Celebratory Choreography:

Similarly audible, two months after the greatest half time show, 'C'mon You Bhoys In Green' was thundered out at Rugby Park. Celtic needed a win to confirm Neil Lennon's first managerial title and the Club's first since Gordon Strachan's penultimate season in charge.

'C'mon You Bhoys In Green' is a choreographed chant that I am sure many readers are familiar with. It originated at Marseille and has been perfected at Celtic. The fans that were housed in the Chadwick Stand, always known to be the livelier of those invariably offered to Celtic supporters, commenced the chant. They willed the Moffat Stand to engage, with gesturing and an indicative cry: "Ohh..." Within a few seconds a roar of "Celtic," had flown from end to end. A volley of "C'mon you Bhoys in green" did the same, with the East Stand joining in too. By the time "Glasgow's green and white" had crossed Rugby Park,

Derek Rae had moved to comment on his bewilderment: "It's rocking now literally, Rugby Park is shaking."

You could not hear anything other than ferocity of Celtic pride bouncing of all confides of the Kilmarnock ground. In the British game it is a style of chant that only Celtic is able to perform so entrancingly. A return to the words of Derek Rae befit the moment in showing how the noise was so gripping: "A little bit of choreography about it as well, you've got the Moffat Stand, the Chadwick and the East Stand – that's where we are situated. Very much in party mode here and they've had to wait so long, four years since the last time. The noise level hasn't really abated throughout this first half."

Here We Go Ten In A Row:
"The fantastic Celtic fans gave a real lesson in civility in sport. The chants and insults which blight too many games in Serie A are light years away from the spectacle of education and sportsmanship that the people in the Celtic away end offered... That horizontal striped white and green jersey is the uniform of a Club worthy of the applause of the world." The above quote is from Xavier Jacobelli, a writer for 'www.calciomercato.com'.

It was March of 2013 and Turin was the venue. On the pitch Celtic were well beaten. Off it, that couldn't be further from the truth. Shortly after the referee blew his whistle to allow Juventus to get the second half underway, the first sound waves of "Here we go ten in a row" were heard. Celtic were undoubtedly going to exit the UEFA Champions League at the last sixteen stage after a gallant campaign. The team had done us proud but the Italian giants were a step too far for the men in green and white. This didn't dampen the two thousand away supporter's enthusiasm though. Even as they broke into a huddle, the chant didn't lose one bit of its aplomb.

After some twenty minutes, a beautiful thing happened – Juventus scored. It's not very often you see the word 'beautiful' and the concession of a Celtic goal together. However, I plead that the goal was linked to one of the proudest moments one can enjoy as a Celtic supporter. Indeed, when Juventus scored, their fans met the strike with a customary cheer. Astonishingly, the Celtic fans didn't miss a beat. Silencing the celebrations, "Here we go ten in a row," was chanted with renewed energy. The ear splitting chant continued fifty four minutes further! This moved the Juventus support to applaud us and some even joined in with the fun.

We Will Never Be Defeated:
In very different circumstances, a fine fight connected to our musical culture took place, in February 2014. Songs of hope and joy, of story and political expression had been deemed "offensive" and led to a number of people being arrested for singing them. As such, 'Fans Against Criminalisation' teamed up with 'The Irish Brigade' to encourage Celtic fans to download the 'Roll of Honour' single online. Paying £1 per download, the money went towards legal costs for those that had been charged for celebrating their heritage in song. The response was outstanding. The song easily made the 'UK top 40'. It even peaked at 24th position in the charts!

'BBC Radio 1' was obligated to play the 'Roll of Honour' in their chart show: "Read the roll of honour, for Ireland's bravest men, we must be united in memory of the ten," sounded from the speakers of radio units across the isles! The achievement showed just what a togetherness and fight the Celtic support can put up. It was one of the most unique moments in the history of any support.

Ronny's First Roar:
2014 ended with yet another special bond being forged at the Club. Ronny Deila had taken over the reign as Celtic

boss and when he took his second placed team to Pittodrie, the pressure was really mounting. As the minutes for injury time were signified and Aberdeen bombarded the Celtic goal; the scoreboard read '1-1'. A welcome break took Celtic up the field and John Guidetti somehow managed to work a corner. Stefan Johansen took the set piece. The ball drifted in through a collection of bodies. Virgyl Van Dijk crept in at the back post and, in a Dennis Law manner, flicked the ball into the onion bag. The Hoops had nabbed the points and therefore, finally reached top spot.

The great moment, for which I write, was when the Celtic team headed to the fans after full time. Unlike most modern day teams, the players and management came right over to the Celtic supporters and actively joined in the celebrations. Ronny Deila ran towards the jubilant crowd in a now trademark, fist pumping frenzy. A return of fan engagement was really good to see and it was a moment that will be cherished long after Deila departs the Club. His first 'Ronny roar'.

A Hero's Goal:
My final special moment is possibly my favourite from the list. It absolutely inspired me and is what confirmed my decision to donate the proceeds from the book to this fantastic Bhoy's charity! Jay Beatty has become something of a cult figure with the Celtic support ever since Giorgios Samaras carried him around the pitch at Celtic Park in 2013. It is testament to Samaras that he kept in touch with Jay and has since met up with him at other times.

Jay was born with Down syndrome in 2003. He is one of the most loving and inspiring people that you will ever come across. His extreme passion for all things Celtic, appreciation of being taken to the hearts' of the support and even his moralities at such a young age is quite remarkable. Evidently, Jay stems from a fantastic family and his father (Martin) appears to have a very close relationship with him.

Indeed, they travel from Armagh to watch Celtic matches together.

The instance that I have elected to conclude with was when Jay's dream came true and he made his Celtic debut! At New Douglas Park on 17th January 2015, Jay was Hamilton Academical's guest of honour for the day. He would enter the home dressing room to wish the 'Accies' players luck before giving a trademark team talk to his heroes in the away changing room. At half time, Jay was invited to make his Celtic debut and to take a spot kick in front of his beloved Celtic fans. He tucked the penalty away with ease and celebrated with a passionate fist pump in front of the roaring support. In Samaras style, he headed for the advertising hoardings with a view to diving into the crowd. Only, they were a little too high for him so he had to settle for the limelight on the field, or so he thought…

The Celtic end broke into song for their hero: "We love you Jay we do, we love you Jay we do, we love you Jay we do, oh Jay we love you!" The moment made national news back in Jay's native Ulster and earned the acclaim of the SPFL, who nominated him for the Goal of the Month award! A landslide victory, with 97% of voters choosing Jay's goal, meant that the Lurgan Bhoy had become the first child to win the honour.

The moment clearly meant a great deal to Jay and his family. Though it also became apparent that he is a member of our family too – the Celtic family: the greatest in the world.

Charlie Mulgrew hands Jay Beatty his Goal of the Month award at Celtic Park – Image supplied by Martin Beatty

The collection of moments that I have chosen are exactly that; just a small collection. There are hundreds more and I apologise for excluding those that failed to get a mention. (There are six further moments that I have reserved for a later section of the book.) It was my intention to convey my enthusiasm for each of my selections and to describe them in the best, most accurate manner possible. Each and every one of you should be commended for making these moments happen, which leads me to my next section, where I hand the baton to yourselves: the stories chapter.

Supporter's Stories

Our stories and our songs are the methods by which generations correspond. Memories that we receive provide the inspiration to travel the Celtic track, from which we experience new mythology to impart on the children of our own.

Celtic fans display fidelity to the Club in a unique way. The anecdotes included in this chapter pay tribute to that and show just why following Celtic Football Club can be such an incredible adventure.

A vibrant support like ours is unsurprisingly enshrined with some entertaining characters. These people are what make following the sacred hoops that bit more enjoyable.

Before heading into some general stories, the tales of those recognisable characters deserve a mention.

The sound of running commentary from the stands is usually very irritating. However, a punter in the Jungle used to do just that at every home game. He would stand at the back of the ash terracing, giving a finely detailed description of proceedings for the benefit of his blind friend. I thought that he was better than the professionals. *(Liam Burt)*

A lady that I remember seeing for many years following Celtic was a lady known as 'Old Betty'. She could be found by the corner flag at the front of the Celtic End, near to the Main Stand side during the 'old' Celtic Park era. She always carried a teddy bear and much to my shock, I saw her once at Motherwell belting out rebel songs! *(Conner Corbin)*

At a game years ago, I remember seeing this guy that looked like Jesus Christ and was carrying a crucifix, for

reasons only known to him. I asked my dad if it was actually Jesus and he laughed like mad. We always used to see him in the Jungle after that. He had the cross and holy modelled look every time.
(Mark Clements)

One of the most loyal Celtic fans of them all is Roddy MacKay. I met Roddy in Milan. He has collected Celtic badges for years, they are all pinned onto his black jacket and total at over a thousand! I asked him how he washes it and he said it takes two hours to get all the badges off!
(Dave Weldon)

There was once a Celtic fan that I used to see at every derby match at Ibrox wearing a full radiation resistant suit and mask! I never saw anyone wearing that at other matches. Suppose you can't be too careful around that lot.
(*Roger Duthie*)

A bloke who used to be seen in the Celtic End never used to pay for travel to any game but still managed to reach the furthest flung locations in Europe. Last time I saw him was in Seville when I got out of a taxi at the fountain and there he was sitting at the bar. He'd hitched his way there, had no ticket but managed to attend the game and get home intact.
(Charlie Taylor)

Everyone knows him now but a friend of a friend of mine is 'Tandoori Tony.' His YouTube songs have been popular but he is better known for his religious dress code at European away games. He's also known as 'Tony pope.' Tony claims to have got his pope outfit in preparation for Halloween! He wore it as a "laugh" to Rennes in the Europa Cup in 2011. The outfit was so well received that it has become an away trip ritual.
(James Reilly)

I don't know him but the biggest Celtic fan is 'Paul the Tim'. Paul never misses a match and that includes qualifiers in Kazakhstan! He also ensured that his mother gave Pope Francis a Celtic shirt when they met and he is the 'official' source of the support for confirming any Celtic news on transfer deadline day. Paul is involved with the Carluke Shamrock CSC I think and he took Kris Common's partner on board the bus for a Scottish Cup match at Dundee. Apparently the last game he missed was back in 2007 in Moscow.
(Paul Pressland)

A guy I always see in the Jock Stein Stand is 'wee' Duff. He always wears green and white hooped trousers and a Jinky shirt, with a hoops poncho type thing on. He wears a hoops hat with badges all over it and carries a sparkling green and white walking stick as well. He's just Celtic daft and is always there!
(Richard Glynn)

I remember a busker in the sixties; he was the biggest con man in Glasgow. He was a disabled man with a bad leg and he used to play the penny whistle. This is the God's honest truth: he used to play songs like the Sash outside Ibrox one week and he'd play tunes like Kevin Barry the next, at Parkhead. Everybody knew what he was up to and we found it hilarious, you couldn't make it up!
(Gerry Duffy)

I was asked to put together a piece about the characters that were involved with Port Glasgow Celtic Supporters No1 Branch. Since the request, I can honestly say that it has been a privilege to have learned the narrative behind the people that shaped the Club. Cheryl Finlay, a friend of mine, kindly chronicled the history of the Supporters Club to which her family has had a connection for almost half a century. I hope that this piece does both the family and story justice.

Registered in 1948, by John Gault (President), Jim McCann (Secretary), Willie Tolan (Treasurer) and Jim 'Digger' Mcculloch (Bus Convener) with the help of Frank Reilly, Jimmy Buntain and Tommy Foster; the Port Glasgow No1 Branch was the oldest Celtic Supporters Club in the town.

The early members showed indefatigable will to raise funds for premises and did so by hosting dances on a monthly basis. Whilst in search of their goal, the members did not lose sight of Celtic's charitable remit. Indeed they put appreciable efforts into supporting worthy causes through a number of other dance nights held at the Town Hall.

Eventually, the Club had sufficient funds to move into four rooms above Monty's Bar, where they remained for some twenty years. During that two decade period, three key men came aboard and directed the Club to new heights. The first, Thomas 'tucker' Mulgrew, joined the Club as a fifteen year old in 1957. He had initially travelled to matches with Arthur Donnachie's Rebel Bus, but having been picked up by the Port Glasgow No1 a lot of times, not least for the famous Coronation Cup Final in 1953; he decided to commit to the latter on a permanent basis.

'Tucker' was first tasked with the unattractive job of protecting the Club board at the back window of the bus! However, he was soon propositioned with becoming Bus Convener, a position in which he excelled. In time, Thomas was running buses from no fewer than four further locations. Coaches from Fife, Edinburgh, Aberdeen and Newcastle ran for home matches, whilst two would be provided for away trips.

The Port Glasgow bus, from which 'tucker' always operated, became known as 'The Chapel Bus' because a number of clergymen travelled with them. Away matches invariably proved the most popular pilgrimage. Life on those road trips entailed a visit to the cinema or the dancing after games. All had to be present for a midnight departure back to the Port, the only condition! The trip of trips was the long jaunt north to Aberdeen. For it was then that the Club would check in to Hasties Hotel for the weekend. Uncannily, the countless journeys with the CSC gave 'tucker' the opportunity to meet a lady named Roberta, who later became his wife.

The next coup for the Club came in the shape of Jackie Dow. Jackie spent many years on the committee, championing the Club's name and playing an instrumental role in oversight of a range of aspects within the organisation. After lengthy service, he abandoned the position to join as a more conventional member. However, his commitment to the community meant that Jackie became the go-to man for ticket collections and related enquiries.

Last of the remarkable trio to join was Hugh Doherty. Aged 21 when he became a member, Hugh dedicated a great deal of time to the Club and ran a number of charitable projects on its behalf. Many ardent fans from the area, were once taken to their first ever match through the Club and it was Hugh who was largely responsible for that. Between lending time to local children and assisting the less fortunate, Hugh gave unequivocal devotion to the Supporters Club. Eventually he was given recognition for his efforts by way of heading the committee.

Under Hugh's stewardship, the group hosted annual bingo stalls for the benefit of Holy Family fetes and St. Vincent's Langbank. He mobilised the Club further and added beneficiaries closer to home when organising member's trips to Portobello and Girvan. In the Presidential role, he both prospered and became synonymous with the Port Glasgow Celtic Supporters No1 Branch. That fact given credence when Celtic Football Club recognised his efforts in the match-day programme on his sixtieth birthday!

Towards the late 1960s, largely thanks to the work of the trinity, the Port Glasgow No1 became the largest registered Celtic Supporters Club in the world! Thus, in 1972 the decision was made to acquire a social club at Fyfe Shore. The property was officially opened by a certain Bobby Murdoch in December that year. The social club was the scene of many a great charity evening, with icons such as Jimmy Johnstone not unfamiliar with guest appearances at the venue.

By the time that the social club was underway, the committee had seen a major overhaul. Peter Mooney headed the Club as President, joined by the aforementioned Hugh Doherty (still in reserve at this time) and Thomas Mulgrew as Bus Convener, Martin Coyle in a secretarial role and Tony Gault in charge of social convening. Of the original founders, only Willie Tolan remained, still in his position as Treasurer.

Just prior to the acquisition of the social club, the Celtic and Rangers Clubs' within Port Glasgow came together to raise monies for the Ibrox Disaster Fund in 1971. It was a strangely companionable evening of dancing at the Town Hall.

A mark of the Port Glasgow Celtic Club was that it was approached by the oldest overseas supporters group, Kearney New Jersey CSC. The American's, led by former Port man (Jimmy Gavin), humbly requested assistance in holding a dinner dance at Fyfe Shore. Of course the committee obliged and the event attracted the attendance of Jock Stein and John McPhail. Jimmy Gavin, President of the Kearney CSC at the time, actually kept in touch with the Port Glasgow Club and his affection for it endured until his passing. He moved back to the Port for a time and was an ever-present on the bus.

In the late seventies, the branch was introduced to St. Joseph's Hospital in Rosewell. After twelve months of supporting, lobbying and collecting for the Hospital; the Supporters Club was able to donate £250. That was quite a sum in those days. The Club was a very sociable group and utilised that facet in moving further to assist the patients in non-monetary form too. This was achieved through arranging Christmas parties for the hospital patients every year.

The ultimate appreciation for the Club's altruistic action was displayed in 1982 when newfound Secretary, Joe O'Rourke (who now acts as General Secretary of the Celtic Supporters Association), relayed a message that he received from St. Joseph's on the Club's behalf. It was that of an official invitation for the Club to meet Pope John Paul at the medical institute. Club President, Hugh Doherty and his wife, Mary represented the CSC proudly. Partnership with the Hospital continued to flourish thereafter. Indeed donations grew to just shy of the £20,000 mark by time that the Club had closed in the mid-1980s. The phenomenal Celtic Supporters Branch sadly met that closure following a string of break-ins at Fyfe Shore.

Today the Club operates as a travel club from the Hibs Hall. Michael Conroy, former Celtic left-half in the fifties and native of the town, is Honorary Club Member. Back when the dances of the early days took place, Conroy was an ever-present. His esteemed position is held alongside an array of Cheryl's relatives within the committee. The trustees include: Hugh Doherty (Grandad) – still as President, Danny Doherty (Uncle) holding down the role of Secretary and Tommy McDade (Uncle) taking charge of Bus Convening duties.

Thomas 'tucker' Mulgrew and Jackie Dow still offer a helping hand, whilst they maintain regular travel to home games. 'Tucker' in fact still embarks on journeys to the away matches as well! Jackie continued to collect match tickets and dedicate himself to that side of the Club for quite some time. Now the oldest member of the Club at the age of 90, he relinquished the responsibility a few years ago!

The persistent involvement of the 'tremendous three' as late as this era is quite astonishing. It's a testament to their love of not only Celtic Football Club, but the Port Glasgow community.

(Cheryl Finlay's story)

Images courtesy of Vagelis Georgariou

Stories:

In Seville as they began running out of beer, a delivery truck was coming in. The masses of Celtic fans crowded in the city, surrounded the truck and the drivers were frightened until the fans all got on their knees and bowed down to the beer at the back. Then they were in stitches.
(Peter Finney)

After the 1965 Scottish Cup Final, as myself (14 years old) and my young brother Jim were exiting Hampden Park down those steep stairways, I noticed there were three elderly gentlemen in front of us, and one seemed full of emotion. He was, in my mind having a hard time getting down the stairs. So I asked if he needed help, "no," said one of his mates "But thanks."

As we proceeded down the slope the elderly gentleman who had been weeping, turned while handing me a ten bob note and said with tears in his eyes, "Son take this, buy you and your pal something for you young uns have something very good to look forward to, I may not be alive to see it but there is something in that team."

Two years later and until today, I have always hoped that, that auld man had lived long enough to witness history.
(Springburn Bhoy)

Finally, it was February 19th 2015. The sound of 'Sean South' from my alarm clock at 6am signified that it was time to get ready to head to Southampton Airport. I put on my Lisbon Lions shirt and grabbed my favourite Celtic scarf from the wardrobe. A four provinces flag was folded and left by the bedroom door but I couldn't be bothered carrying that about and anyhow I needed to hurry up and leave. I grabbed my quality Fred Perry dead 60's tartan jacket and managed to find time for a quick Celtic photograph.

A bacon roll and orange juice slid down in the airport, almost as fast as my money was sliding out the wallet – £5.60! I said goodbye to my family and felt ten feet tall as I went through security, going to see the Celtic on my own for the first time. I was nice and early, so irritated all my Facebook friends with sharing and tagging people in pictures and information ahead of the match. "Flight BE552 to Glasgow, please go to gate 7," said the announcer. I was booed as I took my seat, by a couple of Inter fans. Then it was time to board the propeller plane; the trip had started.

A little over an hour later, I arrived at Glasgow Airport. There, I was greeted by Gerry, who took me to his brother (Brian) that I stay with on my travels north of the border. Both are fantastic people and it'd been a year and a half since our last meeting, so we talked Celtic, mocked the Huns and chatted about my book at length.

My good day was about to get better. It was 4pm and time to make way for The Squirrel Bar in the Barras. After a quick stop at the cash point, I could safely reveal my colours and head to the pub. By then it was 4.20pm and already 'The Squirrel' was mobbed. I pushed the door open to a wall of noise: "Open up your hearts and I'll song for you this song." Glasnevin were playing and an intoxicated Celtic support, giving good vocal back up. After a couple of pints my friends from Port Glasgow had arrived. I had been immensely looking forward to seeing them. A couple of them (John and Aidan) had sat with me at the Ajax game the last season, and I'd not met the other (Kevin) who had kindly sorted my ticket for this game.

Before long, another friend by the name of Ryan and his girlfriend Lynsay, from Paisley had joined us. It was busy so we went to 'The Saracen Head'. We got a table there and that gave us a chance to have a good laugh and chat. They were great guys and girls and I was thoroughly enjoying their company, even if I was being mocked for my 'posh' English accent.

At that point the singing started to get in full swing, as we roared and thudded the floorboards, telling the stories of our heritage. The jukebox played some fantastic Irish songs and Celtic ones too. Everything from 'Rock on Rockall' to 'The Belfast Brigade' was sung with gusto, but best of all was YNWA. We all swayed together and the whole pub was slowly singing along. The noise was deafening when we all passionately raised our voices for the last line: "And you'll never walk alone, you'll NEEEEEE-EEEEE—EEEVVV-EEERRRR WALK all-oo-ne."

The night was still young so with that amazing start we made our way further up the Gallowgate. It was on to Kerry's bar next. I'd never been there and was surprised by how big it was, that's not the first time I would say that on the evening … some size finger on the guitarist! Anyway, some Italians were in the bar with us and seemed to be in awe of the atmosphere. The pub was mobbed and absolutely bouncing. A band played some great tunes for us. Similar to the Sarry, we heard songs ranging from 'The Fields of Athenry' to 'Celtic Symphony'. The atmosphere was phenomenal and the people were great. Myself and my new found pals huddled together to sing 'Over and Over'. You could tell how much we all love Celtic and how drunk we were too. I thought the moment was great and without being a soppy so and so, I appreciated that. These people had sorted me tickets, they'd welcomed me, they'd left work early, taken me up to the Gallowgate and it felt as if I'd known them for years.

There was time still for a truly electric rendition of 'Heat of Lisbon', which went on and on for about five minutes. It didn't abate for a second. Then, after another quick photo and handing of pints to the Italians; it was time to head to Paradise...Or so I thought.

How foolish it was of me to think that the past 150 minutes had provided sufficient drinking time. I should have remembered the tales that a mutual friend (John Davila) had told me about their drinking habits. So it was, we headed to the Tesco in the retail park near the stadium, to stock up on cheap booze, which being a posh Englishman I didn't drink. As I recall, there was also a little Newco Ranger's fan stood outside, collecting for charity. Kevin told him to keep the quid he gave him for himself or better still – his team. I felt sorry for the lad stood there in the rain so gave him a couple of quid and kept quiet. Not that it would have mattered of course but I had just had the micky taken out of me for my swagger and had a feeling there'd be some closet Hun patter forthcoming, so I kept my counsel.

Alas we made way for the Jock Stein Stand. We went into the ground and our tickets were for slightly different areas but we just crammed in, three to a seat. I got the short straw, a cheek to the seats either side of me. Crack inhaling the crisp Glasgow air.

After trying to take in the steepness of Celtic park and the masses of flags all around the ground, it was time for YNWA. My favourite part of a European Night at Celtic Park. Everybody to a man had a scarf aloft, the players were in a huddle and the music stopped. The noise was tremendous and I screamed my lungs out. What a way to introduce the teams to the park. (Picture of this scene on front cover).

Just after kick off, 'Celtic Symphony' had 60,000 people out of their seats and screaming again. The place was jumping. Two quick fire goals from Inter slightly dampened the mood but there were still loud roars of defiance and songs like 'Hey Glasgow Celtic' sung with full participation. I was proud but a bit annoyed in truth. I told another new friend sat next to me, Mcaulay, "This is like Juventus, I was up for that game too." To which he replicd, "Well don't effin' come back again then."

Suddenly, bedlam! It was 2-1 and the atmosphere was mad but hadn't even got going before we grabbed a second. That was just out of this world. I genuinely don't believe any other club produces these moments. The roof came off. Kevin grabbed me and Mcaulay. We and 60,000 others yelled in sheer elation. The celebrations were phenomenal. The period from that ball hitting the net to the 45th minute was crazy. The stadium shook under the weight of the full ground jumping and singing 'Just can't get enough' and 'Hail Hail'. The atmosphere was better than anything that any club in Europe can conjure up. The noise was going right through me and it was just a sight and sound to behold.

Craig Gordon made a howler right before half time to hand Inter the initiative. Craig had been great for us that season so I was full of pride when the entire support sang his name and rallied behind him. Unique to Celtic again and truly faithful through and through.

Half time gave different entertainment. Work this out if you can. My friends and I bought pies and Bovril, totting up to £15 apparently. From a £20 note, we received £22.50 change. Thanks Celtic.

The second half was entertaining and the atmosphere was decent. Every attack was met with an intense roar and there were more electric songs in patches. 'The Fields of Athenry' and the straight forward chant of 'Celtic' being my favourites.

Then when all seemed lost, the ball was looped onto the chest of John Guidetti inside the box. As he swivelled, Parkhead held its breath. "YAASSS!" I've not seen anything like it. Passion like nothing else. I was hugged by Kevin and cuffed round the lug, Mcaulay sandwiched in the middle; we were going crazy. The whole support wern't just celebrating, they were going off their nut. I fell into the man next to me, whom I hugged and roared with before being pulled back towards Kevin and then falling onto the concourse and narrowly avoiding the metal bar in front. I could make out a few bodies flying down the rows. It was incredible. I was so happy to share that moment with my pals and the special support. Kevin said "I wish you could bottle up these moments because they take you to another place." He couldn't be more correct.

We partied in the ground some ten minutes after the game before it was finally time to leave. I headed for Parkhead Cross, fist pumping and scarf twirling all the way. My dad phoned me from home and said he had watched it on TV. He asked how it was to be there. I said "Dad, it's one of the best days of my life, what an atmosphere, what a Club!"

At the weekend I flew home and in the Celtic shop at Glasgow Airport, I met an Irish Bhoy. We were discussing the atmosphere and the Club in general. He said: "I've never experienced anything like it. It's more than a Club, it's a family, it's a community and I love it!" We sat and watched the video of Jay Beatty being named SPFL Goal of the Month winner before I boarded my flight. That was a fitting way to end the trip.
(Liam Kelly - Me)

In 2003, our UEFA Cup Final year, my pal told me that he went on a bus from Shawlands to the Celtic v Blackburn game at Ewood Park. We won 2-0 and so they wanted to celebrate after the match, so they asked the driver to take them to Blackpool. At first he refused and after they had a whip round and gave him eighty quid - he agreed to take them for a few hours. They were in a pub for a few hours and the driver came into the pub and told them to get ready to leave for Glasgow, they had five minutes. They were well p****d and slowly and drunkenly made their way to the bus.

On the bus they were all getting comfy for a wee kip on the way home, when someone from the pub came running out shouting that one of the boys was left behind. They were all ignoring the driver's pleas to go and get him so the driver and a few of the bar staff brought this twenty stone bear of a guy out of the pub. He was drunk and well asleep. They huffed and puffed him onto the bus and laid him on the floor in the aisle between the seats. They didn't really take much notice as they were drunk themselves and trying to get a kip. Thing is, the guy was snoring like a train and about ten miles north of Gretna my pal's cousin woke up asking what the f**k that noise was. As a few more woke up they looked at the lump of a guy on the floor. Some of the guys tried to wake him up but had no luck, then my mate's cousin said that the guy wasn't on the bus coming up to Blackburn.

Anyway, one of the guys had a look for the guy's wallet to see if he had some ID on him. He found a driving license and it had an address in Hamilton on it. So he told the driver to drop him off.

When they got to the guy's house they had to drag him off the bus as he still wouldn't wake up. They managed to get his keys out his pocket and open his front door. They laid him on his couch and left his keys on the mantelpiece and left. They closed the front door behind them and as they were walking down his drive one of his neighbours was coming in from the nightshift and she said: "If you're looking for big Tam, he's away to Blackpool with the wife and kids for a fortnight."

They just nodded and rushed onto the bus and then just wet themselves laughing. They took the bloke home. He must have just seen all the Celtic fans in the pub and thought 'that'll do for me'.

(Username 'zmcfczm')

Back when I sat in the North Stand Upper a few years ago, there was always this guy we'd talk to at the games and every halftime when the paradise windfall numbers came up he'd shout "I've f*****g won, I've f*****g won" and run down the stairs with his 'winning ticket' in his hand. He'd usually return with a pie or a drink or something five minutes later- telling us he was only kidding. It happened every single time there was a game at Parkhead. On one game when we beat Aberdeen late on in the season a couple of years back. He did the exact same thing and ran down to the bottom of the stairs. He was taking an awfully long time on this occasion and we'd wondered what had happened and about a minute after us wondering where he was, he appeared on the field with a cheque for £7,500, giving us the fingers from down on the pitch!

(Nathan)

Most fondly remembered is the unforgettable Macaroon bar seller from the Old Celtic Park. Who could forget the familiar cry? "Get yer Macaroon bars, c'mon Macaroon bars and chewing gum 'ere!" Always a nostalgic topic of discussion, the famous 'Tim' would wander the terraces of 'Paradise' on a regular basis. No doubt, there will be tales in the hundreds but a particularly amusing anecdote stems from a former Jungle wag; who informed me of a day of heart-break. "Gi's yer money ya bassas, c'mon Macaroon bars," the man in question exclaimed. He made his way further up the Jungle in search of sales. Unfortunately his much sought after sales, were not very forthcoming. He burst into a desperate tirade, all the while continuing his climb to the back of the terracing, where he was tripped. Not only did the poor fellow loose his footing but the

contents of his little box had emptied to the floor. Within seconds the bars were hounded by fans, like a pack of dogs. It seemed there was an endless scupper of hands clutching the bars and before long he was totally cleaned out.
(Peter Kilfader's story written on his behalf, by me)

Without doubt this next story is a topper:
The noise of hundreds of Celtic fans singing in unison echoed through the great cavern of Central Station. Saturday shoppers waited stoically for the noisy mob to pass and head for platform 11 where the 'Football Special' waited for them. We soon saw the battered collection of antique carriages British Rail had set aside for us. My old man shook his head, "We're going to Greenock for f**k sake not f*****g Auschwitz," he said as we opened the door of the first carriage, which looked as if it had a little space. The carriage was soon packed with fans and the songs and drink were soon flowing. The last doors banged shut, a whistle blew and the train dragged its tired backside out of Central Station for the short trip to Greenock. Somewhere further up the crowded carriage a flute was playing and the crowd soon filled the carriage with a full blooded rendition of a familiar old song…
"Oh Father why are you so sad on this bright Easter morn, when Irishmen are proud and glad of the land where they were born?"

We all joined in and my old man kept the beat by hitting the table with his hand. When the song was finished he slipped his hand inside his pocket and took out a half bottle of whiskey and took a generous swig. He offered it to my brother and I but we both declined as beer was enough for our young stomachs, especially at lunch time! As the old train clattered and rattled its way towards Greenock the fans in our carriage took turns singing. We heard good singers and bad, Celtic songs new and old, Rebel favourites and eventually a big cheerful, bearded ogre wearing the hoops and carrying a bottle of Eldorado wine looked at my

Dad. "Geez a song auld yin, these young c***s canny sing tae save themselves." My Da' obliged without needing to be asked twice. My Brother and I watched amused as he gestured for quiet before beginning in a surprisingly fine voice…

"They were the men with the vision, the men with the cause, the men who defied their oppressors Law, the men who traded their chains for guns, born into slavery, they were Freedom's Sons."

The carriage was quiet as he sang and somewhere out of sight the sound of a haunting flute could be heard joining my old man in his song. It was a strangely beautiful moment amid the coarseness of the day. He finished to roars of approval and applause and the bearded ogre thrust his wine bottle into my Da's hand, "That was mag-f*****g-nificent," he said, "Have a drink oan me auld yin, yer some chanter so yi ur!" Further up the carriage someone started another song and we all joined in… "Hail Hail, the Celts are here, what the hell do we care, what the hell do we care…" My old man joined in, a pleased look on his face that his singing had been appreciated. He loved following Celtic and filled our away trips with tales from his youth about his various adventures on the road with Celtic. His memories stretched from the near relegation at Dundee in the late 40s, to the 7-1 game. Charlie Tully scoring with two corner kicks at Falkirk to the Coronation Cup miracle. Then of course, there was the heat of Lisbon. We had heard all his stories a hundred times on our long trips following the Hoops and we loved them all. It was our catechism, our heritage, our family history being passed onto us.

The train pulled into Greenock station and the doors burst open and a green and white river flowed through the station towards the exits, shadowed, as always, by lines of unfriendly looking cops and a few fierce looking dogs in tow. As we queued to leave the station, the banter began with the cops. "Aw right big man, ah see ye brought the wife?" one wag in a said, pointing at a huge Alsatian. "Do ye play fitbaw yerself?" He went on. The Cop nodded suspiciously as if waiting for a trap to spring, "Aye, a wee bit." The trap did indeed spring, as the wag went on, "Ah bet yer sh**e though eh?, Bet I could keep a beach baw aff ye in a phone box!" The crowd laughed and, to his credit, so did the cop. We left the station and entered a nearby smoke filled pub my old man knew well. I watched amazed as the local Tims drank wine in pint glasses as if it were water! We spent another happy hour singing and drinking before heading to the game. Morton had a good team back then. Players like Joe McLaughlin, Jim Tolmie and Andy Ritchie always made it tough for Celtic at Cappielow. Ritchie, known as 'Mabawsa' to the Hoops support for obvious reasons, was capable of brilliance on occasion and needed watching. The points would need to be earned today that was for sure. All that day though my old man had been going on about Charlie Nicholas, a young player he had seen playing in the reserves. "Great prospect," he said, "He'll go right to the top that boy!" He had droned on about Nicholas as we queued to get into Cappielow and continued as we found a spot on the terracing at the front and just to the left of the goal. The old stadium was pretty full and the chanting was in full swing. The teams trotted out and much to my Da's pleasure Nicholas was on from the start. The old man fished his big black 'Eric Morcombe' specs out of his pocket and put them on as the game began. Celtic roared forward and were looking good in the opening exchanges. "Nicholas will bag a couple today," my Da predicted confidently. Celtic won a corner at our end and my Da shouted at the bulky 'Mabawsa' Ritchie, "Oot the way fat man, I canny see the game!" The corner was cleared but only as far as Murdo McLeod who fired in a ferocious left foot shot which almost broke the post. We roared for more! Then it happened… A through ball caught the Morton defence square and Nicholas raced

towards the goal with no defender within 10 yards of him. "Come on Charlie Boy!" My Da roared, "Bury it son!" As the Keeper raced out to block him, Nicholas unleashed a powerful rising shot which sped past the post and hit my Da square in the face! He staggered back his specs broken, momentarily stunned! Despite the fact it was my own Da, it was the funniest thing ever. We couldn't contain our laughter and neither could some of the fans around us. My Da however was not pleased, "Ye couldny hit a coo's arse wi a banjo ya useless b*****d!" he began. His tirade of abuse against Nicholas continued for most of the first half much to the amusement of the fans around him.
"Honestly," he went on, "If that f*****g clown was in Dallas shooting at JFK, that man would be alive today!" We laughed our arses off at his caustic comments, particularly as an hour before he'd been singing Charlie's praises. Such was life on the road with Celtic.

Celtic fought their way to a hard won victory on that far off day in Greenock. It was one of those trips which we'd look back at and smile. My Brothers and I would retell the tale to our own kids of the time their Grandad, had been hit by the ball at Cappielow. We told such tales in much the same way he had told us about Tully and Jock Stein. That was the way it was. We handed our stories of Celtic on to the next generation as if it was the most valuable thing we had to give our children. In some ways it was, it was the green thread which ran through the fabric of our lives. It was and is part of us, part of who we are and we should thank those dad's, uncles, and mothers' who taught us to love Celtic. It was a fine gift they bequeathed to us.

Thanks Da… I miss you big man.
(Sent to me by a poster from Cybertims website)

*I have tried to no avail, to contact the person that sent me the above story so that I can put a name to the piece. It is, as an old bearded ogre would say, mag-f*****g-nificent.*

At Hampden for the Cup Final in 1980, when it was still sort of allowed to take a carry out into the game, some guy about forty years old, fell halfway down the stairs - right down at the front of the old terracing in the Celtic end. It was ash on the stairs then, not concrete. Still holding onto his carrier bag, clinking bottles and cans still intact, he said "I'm alright. I'm alright, nay bother." As he was so drunk, he decided to go and lie down for a snooze ten minutes before kick-off.

Everyone around him was kidding on that they were going to nick his bevy! As soon as anyone went near the carryout, he would just roll over on top of it, still sleeping and mumble "Getta fuh ya bassas yur nae getting ma carry oot. Fuh aff."

This Bhoy slept through the full game, extra time, us scoring and going mental all around him, singing like mad all the way through, the cup presentation and a half hour of rioting on the park. Eventually when chaos was brought to order, somebody gave the man a shove and said: "Alright there pal? That's the game finished, time to go home."

The man jumped up still holding his carry out and said "When's the game going to start?" "It's finished pal" he was told.
"What finished? What was the score?" the man replied, startled.
"One nothing to us , George McCluskey."
"Ya f*****g dancer, eeeeeeasy,c'mon the Celtic. Aw I love yeez .F*****g brilliant." The drunk fan yelled.
He started to hand out cans of beer to the boys next to him, and opened up his half bottle of L.D. Eldorado wine. "This is the best f*****g day of my life being here and beating them f*****s in a cup final. Eeeasy. F*****g easy, yeeeeess!" He never saw a thing, but still left as the happiest man in the stadium. Priceless.
(Danny Davis)

I used to work in the Celtic Club on London Road up at Barrowfield. One day on my lunch break I went up to the training ground and looked over the fence at the Lisbon Lions training. They were playing a match and big Jock was refereeing from the touchline. When he blew the whistle everybody had to freeze. Sure enough he blew his whistle and the players all froze. "What the hell are you doing that far deep?" Stein screamed at Jinky. Five minutes later, Jock blew the whistle again and Jinky was again stood in a defensive position. "I told you!" Jock yelled. He chased Jinky the length of the park and booted him full pelt up the backside!

(Gerry Duffy)

I went to see Celtic at Tannadice years back, and there used to be a big massive fence to segregate the fans. On this day, it started as banter but got nasty when all of a sudden our fans were getting pelted with coins and so of course our fans retaliated. It got pretty naughty for a while but it quickly stopped when a man was getting led past all the mad fans with a dart sticking out the top of his head. The place was silent as this Dundonian was getting led round the old track when a voice shouts out "Double tops" the whole stand erupted and even the Arabs were laughing, after that the fighting stopped.

(Dickie)

A few years ago the Green Brigade section were singing Sean South from Garryowen. One boy was getting real passionate but didn't get the lyrics quite correct: "There were men from Dublin and from Cork, Fermanagh and Tyrone but the leader was a leprechaun, Sean South of Garryowen!"

(Davie O'Hara)

As Celtic fan-memories go, I guess we've all stored away millions of little vignettes about away games, Old Firm games, European nights under the floodlights and legendary players doing extraordinary things. That's what we do. Guys have always been collectors throughout the centuries and most football fans are one thing and that's collectors of facts, statistics and mostly (and most crucially) memories.

Where were you when such-and-such scored that last minute winner? Do you remember the time that the superstar player came to a supporters club function and made time for everyone? That much-hated opposition player getting pelters and retaliating with some funny gesture?

We know them, we love them and we particularly love the retelling of them. That is what being a supporter is all about. Those shared experiences with pals, dads, children and partners. These are the moments that really matter as a fan. If you've experienced it, you'll know exactly what I'm talking about. That time that you take your wee Bhoy or Ghirl to their first game; that swelling of the chest as the players appear out of the tunnel; the roar of the crowd as the team bursts out of that huddle and sprint away and the hairs stand up on the back of your neck. And of course, the reliving the experience afterwards; the goals, the penalty incident or the blind, opposition-supporting referee who's brother is in The Lodge. It's called making our own legends and history, and it's something we, as Celtic fans, excel at.

The story I have to tell is one of those. It's a cataclysmic moment in Celtic's recent history and do you know what? I wasn't even there!

It's 1998. May the 9th. An early kick off and Celtic know that a win against St. Johnstone at home will win the title and stop Rangers and their seemingly inexorable march to 10-in-a-row, beating the long-held Celtic record of nine. Wim Jansen had arrived with very little fuss or excitement the year before but against the odds (and despite the Scottish media trying and failing to make the man a laughing stock), Celtic had pulled themselves into contention and had won a first League Cup in some years the previous November.

Rangers had been beaten by Aberdeen a few weekends before whilst Celtic had inflicted a mauling on Motherwell. The week after these crucial games, Celtic had drawn with Hibs whilst Rangers had beaten Hearts 3-0.

Tension and excitement was palpable amongst the Celtic support but many thousands more had seen and witnessed too many false dawns and almost expected the team to fail at the last hurdle. It seemed to be becoming yet another "seen-it-all-before" when despite Rangers dropping points at home in the penultimate game, Celtic could only manage a tense draw the following day at East End Park with Dunfermline equalising late on. Hearts in mouths time again.

It was a familiar tale; Celtic getting so far and either some mishap, or more often, the bottle crashing at some crucial moment would see The Hoops pick up the second prize as the seemingly never-ending party down Govan way continued apace.

I had a season ticket. I'd been at almost all of the games that term. I'd been up, down and all-around as Celtic stumbled, picked themselves up and quietly ground down the gap between ourselves and Rangers. It all came down to this and I couldn't go.

My 18 month old daughter Caitlin required that her Dad stay at home that day and so it was TV time for the Bhoy Whyte. I had invited my best mate round; he'd no ticket either and as the sun blazed down, we wandered around the house chewing the tips of fingers and nails as countdown to kick-off approached. The wee yin was as good as gold as she kept us laughing in her "Caitlin 7" hooped top with Henrik Larsson "running-pointing/tongue-out" goal celebration impersonation and endless questions.

The game kicked off. It was one of those beautiful days that seem made for title parties. Watching the TV coverage is always tenser than actually being there. It's almost like you're in a solitary little bubble of your own anxieties despite the company around you. Listening on radio is even worse. One can hear the swell of the crowd a second or two before the commentary and you know something good or bad has just happened. Celtic are controlling the game but we've been here before. The notorious "sieve" of the Celtic defence is always a concern despite the teams' attacking prowess. Nerves were slightly settled when Henrik cuts in across the St Johnstone 18-yard line from the left, sells a couple of defenders with a deft shoulder drop and unleashes a curling shot that sends Celtic Park into paroxysms of relief and delight when it hits the back of the net.

Weirdly, in the mists of time, it's the second goal that is always credited with "stopping the ten" but personally I think that the Larsson goal settled the team down and let Celtic start to play with a bit of confidence. As it arced in off of Henke's right toe, myself, Caitlin and mate Peter are terrifying the neighbours as we take off out of the back door shrieking "goooooooooooooooooal!!!!!" at the top of our voices.

Taking our seats we open more beers and wait for the deluge. No chance. This is Celtic Football Club. Nothing is EVER that simple. St Johnstone start to play and the Celtic players are making unforced errors, hitting misplaced passes and the crowd get antsy and restless as the body language of the players starts to look a little anxious.

George O'Boyle, the St Johnstone (and NI) player is taking lots of stick from the fans but he nearly inflicts heart-stops on the massed ranks with a near-miss in the second half. Donnelly is replaced with the misfiring Harald Brattbakk with about a quarter to go. The Celtic fans, as they so often do, have taken the hard-grafting (and obviously gifted) Brattbakk to their hearts and really, really want him to succeed but with every passing game, he's looked like more of a misfit and couldn't hit the proverbial coo's erse. Trying to keep ourselves from psychological meltdown, Pete and I are slugging the beers like they're going out of date. The ex-wife has returned and Caitlin has relinquished the football for the moment. She probably couldn't stand the sight of two grown men gritting their teeth and pacing the floor to be honest.

Myself and the bold Pete are having a bit of a laugh about former wing back Tosh McKinlay, whom Scotland manager Bertie Vogts had described as "a specialist". We both thought he specialised in one thing- running aimlessly about quite fast.

In that same position today was Jackie MacNamara, a young guy who had made quite the impression at right back. Tom Boyd, the skipper, won the ball and made a rare surging upfield foray. He rolled the ball to MacNamara who steamed forward down the line as the old "Jungle" rose in anticipation. Galloping through the midfield was Brattbakk who simply stroked the ball home from MacNamara's arrowed cross. The explosion of relief and sheer ecstasy from the Celtic support was almost equalled by the two forty-year olds knee-sliding across the living room floor and hugging each other in joy before our normally-reserved "Scottish bloke" personas returned and we sat in stunned silence for a few minutes. The ref blew the whistle and the party was in full swing in the East End but here in Bishopbriggs, an exhausted hush took over. That only lasted five minutes. The next sight to behold was two drunken guys and a wee curly-headed tot in the back garden recreating the Brattbakk goal. Over and over. And over.

Later in that pre-broadband/social media day, we heard some great tales of Celtic fans converging on all the motorway bridges from Deeside down to Glasgow with hastily-made banners "congratulating" the Rangers fans and players returning from their fruitless final day at Dundee United.

These, shared with family and friends, are the type of memories that make being a Celtic fan special.
(Joe Whyte)

In April 1970 on an old fashioned train somewhere outside Leeds, two suits with Scottish accents went through the Celtic team that had just beaten Leeds Utd at Elland Rd 1-0 in the European Cup Semi-Final. Every Celtic player's faults were mentioned, when eventually my old man says "Hold it a minute, you've just taken apart a team that's gone away to a European Cup Semi-Final and won."

"Okay" says the older man, "let me and you go through the team if you know so much."
Two hours solid the guy chatted to my old man about Celtic players. The penny dropped with my old man that this geezer (who he couldn't quite place) was fishing about players. The other guy said nothing. The quiet man was Ron Yeats, captain of Liverpool. The other was a certain football manager called Bill Shankly. Total football.
(Drumchapel CSC)

John Spencer, who used to run a CSC bus, travelled on the Govan Emerald to many an away game in Europe, but vs Young Boys, he was dressed in a suit and tie which he had slept in since Govan. Outside the ground everyone thought it would be best if he was left on the bus to sleep off his drunken state, apart from Spencer who woke up just before kick-off strolled right up to the main door at the stadium and showed his library card, claiming to be a Celtic official. He walked straight into the game.

(Govan Emerald CSC)

I was over in Teplice on a bus in 2004. We had spent hours on the coach and I just wanted to get off and grab a pint. In my rush, I forgot to find out the meeting point after the match. It was minus 22 degrees and after full time, I was lost. I couldn't find the bus anywhere! I walked about alone absolutely freezing and came to a crossroads. I looked left but for some reason turned right instead. Then this bus full of Celtic fans drove by. It stopped at the end of the road and a couple of guys gave me the w****r sign saying "Colin we've been looking for you for ages and were about to give up, get in ya clown!" Thank goodness I bumped into them – I almost walked the opposite direction.

(Colin Black)

Colin is a friend of mine from Chris Sutton Southampton CSC. He is absolutely nuts, but a great man and massive Tim!

For my 19th birthday, I went with a few of the Chris Sutton Southampton CSC members to see Derek Warfield & The Young Wolfe Tones at Portsmouth Irish Club. It was a great night. Colin moved an old man from his bar stool so that he could have a seat, because he had shattered his heel a few weeks before. The next minute he was up dancing when they played 'Broad Black Brimmer'. The old guy comes over and says: "What's that about your heel then?" "It's a Glaswegian thing!" Colin said and burst into laughter.

Throughout the gig, we had all been filling Colin's coat pocket with beer mats, without him knowing. We got a taxi back to the train station to return to Eastleigh. Colin went to pay the driver and reached into his pocket only for his face to drop as he pulled out beer mat after beer mat. No sign of any money. We were killing ourselves in the back seats. Colin just stood in silence.

After we put Colin in the picture, we got on the train and that's where the real fun began. Firstly, a man from Portsmouth got on and saw us with all our Celtic shirts, whilst holding Irish CDs and Wolfe Tone books. He looked puzzled and said: "Where was Celtic playing today? If not down here, what are you all doing here? Wait so you are English and Scottish, supporting a Scottish team but you went to an Irish gig? I'm confused. Is this Celtic as in Glasgow Celtic, am I right?" With that, Colin nudged the man aside, gave a conductors gesture and shouted: "Forget him! Let the people sing their stories and their songs." All six of us jumped about and sang along. Then said Portsmouth bloke popped back up: "I don't get it but all I will say is you sing and you sing very well!"

Being the character that Colin is, he created another moment of laughter. He had spotted a teenage girl sat on her own in the same train carriage, so he took a seat opposite. With genuinely innocent intention, he sat down and said: "'Awrite pal?" She was taken aback at being spoken to by a drunk Glaswegian stranger on the train at 1am! She just returned the question. Colin clearly hadn't taken the hint: "Yeh cool in the gang, we've just been to see 'The Wolfe Tones.'" "I don't know them!" She blurted before turning away and plugging her headphones in. Colin looked like a lost puppy. After a moment's reflection, he sprung to life: "Silly cow!" he said, cackling with his distinct drunken chuckle; "We're on the one road sharing the one load, we're on the road to God knows where." The One Road is our CSC favourite and the drunken dancing highlighted that.

Uncannily, a lady from Virginia (USA) with her ex Royal Navy husband, walked to our carriage at this time. Clueless to the lyrics, she clapped along and whistled. We all rallied up everybody on the train, well all of us except Colin. He was away touching knuckles with the 'silly cow'. The efforts of the rest of us (Scott, Richard, John, Frank and me) had taken effect in minutes and the carriages were bouncing. Things calmed down and we got chatting to the lovely couple. The male was a Villa fan and we goaded him into giving us a song. "Villa, Villa, Villa, Villa." His effort was shocking. We told him as much and he reckoned we couldn't sing anything without it being political. Rather than bite, Scott started "Country roads take me home to the place where I belong." Colin's eyes lit up, not dissimilar to the change in a darkened room as the lamp is switched on: "WEST VIRGINIA" he shouted with a smile as wide as the train track, pointing to our Virginian friend. It was a song that everyone knew and the husband and fellow passengers alike used it to make her embarrassed.

The Navy man's comments about our songbook were bugging me so I started off 'Willie Maley' to disprove his claim. By the time we had reached 'Murdoch, Auld and Hay' for the third time, Colin interjected. Sharply, he yelled: "STOP!" Everybody fell silent and panicked. Then a wry smile grew on his face, "Tickets please!" He jokingly said. We were in raptures.

Back at the train station, we bid a fond farewell to all aboard. I spoke briefly to the Virginian lady and suffice it to say we have a new fan. She was gripped by my short narrative of the Club.

Only Celtic can bind people like that!
(Liam Kelly –Me)

This happened years ago at Rugby Park. For some reason I ended up going to watch Killie in the home end with my big pal who's always been Killie daft.

Anyway half time comes and everybody piles into the pie queue, we get back to our seats just before the second half starts. two or three minutes after the half kicks off there's a commotion to the right of us a couple of rows in front, but it's only a massive guy returning late from the food kiosk, with four pies balanced on top of each other in one hand, cup of tea/coffee in the other. After upsetting the whole row by taking ten minutes to squeeze past everyone he eventually sits down, two pies balanced on one knee, one on the other knee and the other already under attack in his hand.

We were behind one of the goals, slightly to the left and maybe a dozen rows back. Killie win a corner, cleared by the defence and it comes to Durrant (I think) at the edge of the box, who puts the guttie through it. It looked in all the way and it was travelling like a cannonball. Sadly for those Killie idiots (Chris excluded) it flew high and handsome. And skelped the huge chap square on the coupon as he was taking a bite of his pie. The mess was surprising, we were both hit by bits of meat and Christ knows what else. But the funniest bit was the genuine emotion the big guy showed, he actually cried. The other pies that were balanced on his knees fell as he jumped when the baw scudded him. The greedy git still ate one of them.
(Dresden 79)

I love away days. The journey, the craic, the bevy, the singing… the bus makes it. I went down to Ipswich on a Tuesday night in November 1981 for Alan Hunter's Testimonial. I went down with the Johnny Thompson bus and we used to do a pick-up in Renfrew, so the bus was also known as the Renfrew Rebel bus as well. It was crazy.

We had some laugh that night. At the game itself, the flood lights conked out due to a flood of weak bladders! Everybody had been doing their thing at the foot of the flight lights and it caused a power cut. Somehow, 'The Wolfe Tone flute band' from Wishaw were providing the entertainment. They were parading about in the dark for ages whilst the second half was delayed.
(Fred McNeill)

I checked this out with Fred online and found that everything that he had recollected was accurate. We found a host of interesting information about the match too. Firstly, the ticket cost just £1.50. Celtic won the match 3-2 with a McGarvey goal in the 88th minute, having conceded in the 87th! Ipswich were UEFA Cup champions at the time. Five thousand Celtic fans travelled down. The police wrote a letter to Billy McNeill to compliment the Celtic fans on their behaviour.

We also found the following quotes: "Those Celtic fans are bloody marvellous people!" – Sir Bobby Robson (manger of Ipswich at the time). "Down here they talk about Liverpool but they are not in the same class as those from Glasgow. Celtic have the best support in the world." – Alan Hunter.

Another story is from before my time. My father in law from Barrhead used to tell me about a story he was told, regarding a time when Celtic opened Arthurlie Juniors Park. The story goes that Celtic were two players short and drafted in two locals. They lost the game I think, though my father in law always said Celtic won.
(Fred McNeill)

When we looked this one up, we found that the game took place in January 1897. It was a Scottish Cup first round tie and Celtic only had seven first team players available due to 'accidents and suspensions'. They had to draft in four reserves. The reserves were awful. Our first ever captain, James Kelly, won the toss and chose to kick downhill first! A large crowd of 'local enthusiasts' had come to Dunterlie Park to see the match. The final result was a 4-2 victory for Arthurlie over Celtic, which given the circumstances wasn't too bad for us. However, the following season we drew them in the cup again and had a full team available. We won that encounter 7-0.

My recollections of supporting Celtic in the 40s are of my older brother, God rest him, desperately trying to get more money for us by busking outside the stadium. He could only sing three songs: 'Johnny Thompson' (not the song about him today), 'Dear Little Shamrock' and 'Faith of Our Fathers'. I still remember the night we had when we went with Dad up to Dundee after the war and Celtic nearly got relegated. We celebrated back at home as we didn't have money to do much else. My brother sat in the lounge and sang for us all night. He had added 'Soldier's Song', 'A Nation Once Again' and 'Slieve Na Man' to his repertoire by then.
(Bertie Maccarick)

In the fifties and remember there was no Jungle at this time, as we knew it. We used to go behind the goal for songs. Singing wasn't the same as now but it could still be very good, it just wasn't as frequent. Anyway, my memories are singing about the Border Campaign. Life was very hard back then for Catholics. Remember this was also a time when 'No Irish Need Apply' signs and cartoons were made in the media. So going to Celtic games was a real relief. We would read the Irish news and learnt a lot about the situation back 'home'. That's why when 'The Troubles' kicked off we were well clued up. Anyway, I just remember one occasion we all sang 'Sean South of Garryowen' constantly for the first half. Then in the second, it was the 'Soldiers Song'. Fantastic memories.
(Fergal Callahan)

My greatest ever memory was back in 1957. I was working as an apprentice with a whole host of Rangers fans. They were nice to me but beneath it, they were bitter gits. They offered to tell my ma that they wanted to train me at the weekend, which was very unusual. This was so that they could take me to the League Cup Final. I thought it would be ok but when we went to the pub and they started all their nonsense I regretted it. The boss made me stand at the front of the bus and sing Irish songs, whilst they mocked me.

Once we got into the ground and Celtic started scoring more and more, all the Huns started rioting among themselves and throwing bottles at each other. I was terrified so I ran with my hands over my face down to the front. Then I pulled my Celtic scarf out of my pants and showed it to the police officer, who took me round to the Celtic fans. I had been listening to the thousands in green and white singing 'Hail Glorious Saint Patrick' and cheer every touch. Now finally, I got to be among it. I had to walk home that night and face the wrath of my parents when I was so late getting in. No mobiles in them days. The trouble was very bad against Rangers in them days as well.

I went in to work laughing on Monday morning. Five minutes later I got sacked!
(Michael Brennan)

In the 60s up at Airdrie, a dog ran on the pitch. The whole Celtic end started sing 'There's only one John Greig.' It was a good quick bit of patter.
(Joseph Devine)

In the Old Celtic Park everybody used to pee in cans or on the floor because it was so crowded and because everyone was downright dirty. One time this guy was handing out a few cans and people were thanking him until someone takes a sip and it was full of urine.
(Pete Duffy)

I remember after a game at the old Hampden against Rangers, we had to cross paths leaving the stadium. It was a ridiculous set up. "He's got a gun!" Somebody shouted and we sprinted as fast as we could, the dust kicked up was incredible, I couldn't see a thing. Apparently one of the Rangers fans had a shotgun that he pulled out from a rucksack. Nobody was hanging about to find out.
(Pete Duffy)

I went with my older brother (Pete) to a game at Ibrox for the first time. We had our Celtic scarfs on and I followed Pete leading up to the ground. "You idiot!" I said in fear. We were soon surrounded by Rangers fans singing all the usual bile. One Rangers fan came over to us tucked our scarfs inside our coats and said: "'Mon boys you shouldn't be at this end, here go this way round to your lot and hurry." I've never been so afraid but he was dead good to us.
(Brian Duffy)

In 1992, can't mind who we were playing but we were a couple of goals up at half time at home and ended up losing the game. The Jungle just burst into an absolute song fest, not caring what was happening on the park and just celebrating everything that was good about Celtic (which wasn't much at the time). This continued all the way back to our bus and then on the bus. We were crawling back through Alexandria parade and the bus was rocking, defiance was ramped up to ten. Anyway loads of Tims were walking along the Parade and one of them looks up to the top deck (where we were) and starts singing along with us and giving us the clenched fist in solidarity. Bold yin on our bus is feeling the connection with the guy, slides open the wee windae (old style double decker with wee slide along windows) and squeezes himself as far as he can manage out the windae to start singing the soldier song along with this guy on the street, real passionate stuff.

Anyway, the daft fool gets stuck in the windae. We had to get the fire brigade to come and get him out.
(Sean Daleer)

I used to sit in section 113 and in the seat next to me was the biggest idiot you could ever meet. I had to listen to his whinging all season long so at the end of the campaign I decided that I was going to relocate. I moved to the Jock Stein lower section 141 and was excited for the season ahead. When I took to my seat for Flag Day, I got chatting to the new guy that I would sit beside and told him why I relocated. It came out that the idiot at the other end of the ground, the previous season, was his brother! Not only that, but his brother had relocated to be beside him as well. Sure enough, five minutes later, he arrived so I had to put up with the two of them!
(Eamonn Flood)

Against Rangers in 2012, Kyle Bartley picked up the ball and a bloke at the back of the North Stand screamed: "Get into the unwashed b*****d!" Instantly, a squeaky voice from a young Hoop replied: "which one?"
(John Symonds)

Ibrox in the late 80s we went to buy a pie at half time and a Celtic fan sprinted to stop us. He screamed at the guy in front "Don't buy a proddy pie! Bobby Sands went days without food and you can't last ninety minutes!"
(Mark Wood)

I was one of the fortunate 80,000 travellers to Seville that had been successful in the ballot so the next stage for me was securing flights and accommodation. This was to prove challenging, but in the end a good friend of mine had managed to find a charter flight and hotel that would accommodate our group which would travel out on the Tuesday afternoon and return to Glasgow on Thursday evening.

Travelling separately from me was my father and his group, who decided a week long excursion in the Portuguese holiday resort of Albuferia would be a suitable base camp and only a two hour drive to Seville. Now one of the group decided that they would forge one of the tickets to ensure the rest of the group would have a match ticket in the event that the stewarding was relaxed…more about that later.

So the day of travel had finally arrived and we made our way to Glasgow Airport and as we approach the airport you had to wait in lines outside the airport entrance before checking in,if I recall I think we gave ourselves at least four hours lead time as we knew there might be some queues but this was unbelievable. Thankfully the airport staff were prepared and we finally checked in and made our way to the departure lounge for a much needed refreshment!

It wasn't too long before we boarded our plane and sitting only a few rows from the back I was praying that the drinks trolley wouldn't start from the front. Once again we would not be disappointed, as the air steward appeared from the back of the plane with a full complement of refreshments. During that three hour flight I don't think the air steward made it passed ten rows as cries from the back requesting more drinks had her constrained. One other bonus on this flight was the sight of Derek Whyte and Willie Falconer seated only a few rows away and they gladly accepted the adulation given to them in song by the supporters…well everyone was in a good mood.

Once landed in the searing evening heat of Seville, my goal was to meet up with my father as I had already decided before I left that this may be the final time he might see Celtic in a European final and I wasn't going to let him watch from a TV screen. We finally met up and after a few beers we headed back towards his hotel to a nearby bar. I presented him with my ticket he was overjoyed and it made me feel that I had given something back to him.

Now the game was on to acquire another ticket or several for that matter as my own group were needing tickets. We decide the best course of action was to wait until a couple of hours before the game and send those with tickets up to the ground to scramble for more, while those without waited patiently at the hotel for the phone to ring. It was a forty five minute walk from our hotel to the stadium so our patience was running thin as time passed, but once that phone rang to inform us that five tickets had been purchased for €150 Euros a piece, the journey to the stadium was on.

We knew the tickets that had been purchased were for the Porto end of the ground but that didn't matter and the price paid equated to the cost of a Porto season ticket so you can understand why some of their supporters were willing to give them up. As we made our way around to the turnstile we knew that we couldn't hide our colours so would we be refused entry. That obstacle hadn't really occurred to us before then, but as we approach the perimeter we could see several Celtic supporters lining up at our turnstile so the omens were good. We agreed with a few others in line that we should try and congregate in one area as close to the Celtic end as possible, however as we made our way along the concourse we realised some supporters managed to obtain access to the Celtic end, but as we approached the gates closed, so we decided to assess our options from the seated area. Once there, we noticed that we could climb over a six foot Perspex barrier into the Celtic end, so the five of us including a friend's father approaching his sixties, dashed up and over before anyone could notice and into the confines of our own.

Remember those forged tickets I was telling you about? Well, each ticket was bar-coded and scanned at the turnstile, the owner of the real ticket was refused entry as his ticket had already been scanned, and the culprit has never been found. His brother who was with him wasn't going to go down without a fight and seeing an opportunity present itself, he walked up to a supporter in a wheel chair being pushed towards the gate that was being opened for him and grabbed one end of the chair and calmly walked into the stadium...result!

These memories will live with me forever and strengthen my belief that I support the greatest football club in the world.
(Davie Calgary CSC) – Initially sent in by Tommy Fulton, who is the unfortunate person whose genuine ticket was denied.

I have really enjoyed my journey following the Club to date and look forward to doing the same for many years to come. The best part is definitely the away European matches and especially the gigs that I would acquire in the different locations around the world including Amsterdam, Milan, Bucharest and Croatia.

I have met and made many new friends through my music and the Celtic connection and this has given me some of my best memories to date. The fact that you are travelling with the best behaved football supporters in the world and every country recognises that as well, is extra special.
My best memory, no doubt has to be being allowed to play on board a Ryanair Flight coming back from Bucharest along with another group of musicians who were flying over to Dublin for a gig. I had been out in the city most of the day singing and consuming a few beverages so by the time the flight took off we were well juiced. But the flight attendants let us up the front of the aeroplane to perform a few tunes and everyone on the plane really soaked up the atmosphere - this was 30,000 feet in the air.

I have never seen this happen in my life and especially the flight attendants videoing us on their phones. I then did a bad job of trying to sing 'Caledonia' through the intercom

system, another first to happen on any flight. All can be seen on YouTube. I just hope the poor souls still have their jobs…. if only all flights were like that one.
(Damien Quinn)

My pals and I were going to a Scottish Cup Final against the Rangers many moons ago, on a coach from Dumfries. It broke down on the M74, so everyone started hitching lifts. This car pulls up and said 'I can take three of you.' So we jumped in the back. To our surprise Alex Ferguson was in the passenger seat and his son, Darren, was driving.
(William)

I played pairs golf in Dorset at a nice club. We got drawn against a pair, one of which was called 'Hastings'. He was a Kilmarnock fan and my son had bought me a Celtic driver cover a few weeks before. I mentioned it to 'Hastings' and he was very bitter about it. He started saying about all the Rangers buses that leave Kilmarnock still and kept slagging us. It was driving me mad. Half way into the round, I lost the driver cover. I looked at him and he said: "I haven't touched it, I'd of smoked it if I got it."

At the last hole, he put a lovely shot on the green. He was celebrating, thinking that he had won it for his pair. I was determined to win. I chipped the ball with a pitching wedge from about ninety yards. It was well lofted but it bounced right into the tree behind the green, miles from the flag. Then it ricochets off to the slope at the bunker and somehow rolled back down before stopping right by the flag. It was a 'gimme' putt. In the clubhouse he blamed my head cover for the loss. I just went over to him and said: "Celtic won 2-0. I don't know how Kilmarnock got on." I knew full well that they had lost 4-0. I booked to play against him in the singles the next Saturday.
(Ian Kelly)

When the Club had reached the last sixteen of the UEFA Champions League for the very first time in 2006, AC Milan were the opponents and an incredible support of over the sixteen thousand mark headed to Italy! Most supermarkets sold out of beer because of the party mood of the support, largely gathered in Duomo Square. The atmosphere seemed to travel down each avenue of the beautiful streets nearby, laced with magnificent architecture. The game itself ended in heartbreak with a late extra time goal from Kaka robbing the win for AC. Not all was lost though.

Off the park Celtic fans had earned the respect and applause of the Italians for their constant singing of 'Willie Maley' throughout the first half. Then, having been beaten, they showed such wonderful humility in playing 'Midnight five-aside' as it was called, with the locals! The on tour Hoops hosted a penalty shootout back at the square; something many felt they should have witnessed back at the San Siro instead. The sheer brilliant quality to raise our spirits was shown when Japanese tourists were offered piggy backs to humorous chants of "Nakamura" and "There's only one Nakamura, one Nakamura, he eats chow mein, he votes Sinn Fein, walking in a Naka' wonderland!"
(John Donoghue's story)

In Lisbon a few years ago, we were drinking in the Irish bar down beside the river packed full of 'Tims' and outside there were loads of locals out jogging. My mate goes for a wee. Next thing we see are these two stunners out on a jog, as they pass, Davy appears from the bog with nothing on but a green and white jester's hat and a pair of runners holding a tri colour; and proceeds to jog after them. The look on their faces as he jogged past them singing the 'Celtic Song' was priceless.
(Mr. Duffy) *Not a Duffy that I know for a change!*

I could tell stories all day every day about being a Celtic supporter, especially since the 'Lennymobile' was born. When I attended my first Celtic game in Tampa, in 2000, after the game all the Celtic fans went to a pre-arranged location. It was a small bar in Tampa with hundreds of Celtic fans outside. They were selling six packs for $20, which was damn expensive. I bought one and asked another Celtic fan to keep an eye on it, while I ran back to my hotel room to get something. "No problem," he says. When I returned, he was gone and my friend laughed that he was off with my 6 pack. I said "There's no way that another Celtic fan would do that." I looked around and right near where we were standing; I spotted a bush and looked inside. There was my six pack, untouched!

In 2004 I went to Philadelphia (Eagles new stadium) to watch the 'Bhoys' play Man united. The stadium was sold out with over 40,000 people. I was in the fourth row at the corner. Anyway, early in the game, a guy next to me in the crowd recognised me from somewhere. I replied: "You probably saw me at other Celtic games." Then it came to him and he asked: "Did you get that six pack ok in Tampa?" At half time we had a few drinks and I thanked him dearly.
(Martin Smyth – owner of the 'Lennymobile')

Probably the funniest thing I have ever seen in my life was against Aberdeen. A Couple of wee guys behind us were shouting daft things like "Away and shine yer nut ref!", "That whistle must have been a birthday present" etc... All of a sudden this guy a few rows in front who had obviously been listening to them for a while before standing up and, in the most serious, poisonous tone of voice I`ve ever heard shouted, "Aberdeen, Aberdeen, couldnae kick a Jelly Bean!!!" And sat down again to the sound of everyone around him p*****g themselves laughing!
(Stephen Dennie)

Mid-way through the first half at Brentford, the ball rolled innocuously out of play for a goal kick. Suddenly a fan leaps the barrier and strolls up to the ball. He opened his foot and took the goal kick before jogging to the corner flag and eventually jumping back into the Celtic support.
(Des Upton)

I have a story of my own from the Brentford v Celtic game in July 2013. We finished lunch at McDonalds and turned the corner back on to the main Ealing Road, when a Celtic fan swaying all over the shot managed to ask us where the nearest McDonalds was - oblivious to the huge golden arches sign overhead! He then bemused me and my friends by pulling out some elastic bands and playing cards. "Let me show you a few tricks please?" he asked, we obliged curious of what was going on.

He opened out the pack and allowed us to pick any card we wished, re-inserting it anywhere we wanted after a quick look. He managed to find our card from the pack every time without fault: with his eyes closed and the cards shuffled. He repeated a sheepish look and simply stated exactly which card we had, over and over again until we could stand no more. I was more impressed by his elastic band skills though. He placed a band over my finger and demonstrated to us that the only way to remove it was to take it back over the top. My friend prevented him from doing so by putting his hand on top of my finger. This magician then flicked the band with his thumb and first finger and suddenly it was in his hand, in one piece; I was discombobulated. I sought an explanation but he ran straight off to McDonalds and thanked us for our participation.
(Liam Kelly -Me)

In Portugal for the Benfica game a couple of seasons ago, a load of us got the train from Albufeira to Lisbon. This guy that looked like Will.i.am, got on with a guitar and we asked for a few tunes. He started singing 'Sit down next to me' and he was great. We had a laugh singing with him. "Oh sit down, oh sit down, sit down next to me, sit down, down, down, down dowwwwn…" Then one of the Celtic fans ahead took the singer's hat and replaced it with a green, white and gold balaclava. The guy just kept on singing with this balaclava on, clueless as to what it was about. One of the blokes on the train recorded it and I found the video on YouTube the other day. It's called 'Celtic fans on Lisbon train' for anybody wanting a look. It's worth it just to see how good the singing was, if not for the laugh.

(Written on Marian Hearney's behalf by me)

I remember watching Rangers against Cologne on TV. I knew it was in the seventies and a Google search shows that it was 1979. I think a feller from my scheme, Jim Denny, was playing for 'them' at the time. I just remember in the middle of the game Rangers were on the attack and suddenly Jesus Christ on the cross appears on the screen! It was meant to be an advert for half time but they got the timing wrong. The station was inundated with Rangers fans going mad and complaining. It was a cracker!

(Fred McNeill)

At McChuill's, the boozer was full so everyone partied outside. There was a large queue with the usual songs then someone above the bar started throwing chips at us. We stepped out the queue shouting "Pr**ks," only to see that it was actually a pigeon on a window sill eating left overs in the usual pigeon way, lift and flick!

(Bowie)

When I went to Seville, I was 22. My boss, who was a big Rangers fan, was just not up for letting me go. It got to about a week before and I was in the pub. My friend and his dad said: "We are booking up to Portugal and need an answer now if you want to go." The next morning the three of us booked up. We stayed in Portugal and it seemed every pub in the area was an Irish bar. They were not daft and even the nightclubs were playing rebel music into the small hours. The morning before the match, I had to make a call to work. I found it difficult to sound ill as I was buzzing like you could not believe. It was very noisy outside and someone decided to do a divebomb in the pool. I just said "Jenny stop bouncing about in that bath I'm on the phone." It seemed to work… I think. The night before that call, I got wasted and ended up walking home with a girl I had pulled and her younger brother. The girl and I were holding hands and started running down to the beach. At this point I got caught up and before I knew it we were naked, our Celtic tops were off and we were rolling about the sand. She had sand in her mouth and I had sand in every crevice possible. Her brother ended up coming down some moments later with two policemen with torches. The both of us decided to make a swim for it. I jumped in the sea and started swimming to try and lose the officers. As you can imagine I was not going to get very far and the policemen just followed me down the beach for a few moments shining there torches in my direction. I'm sure they were laughing. Anyway, after I gave myself up they handed me some leaves to cover myself and said "Go home now." At this point I had no idea where my clothes were. Then I got lost! For the life of me I could not remember the name of my hotel. I waited for a while under cover and then asked some locals for some clothes to cover up. Two kind men gave me a shirt and t-shirt. I wrapped the shirt round my bottom half and put this t-shirt on. I started walking and by this point I was way into local territory. I had no money, no phone, nothing. I remembered the hotel my family were at but this was miles away. I was f***ed!

I started walking again and noticed a bunch of holidaymakers from the UK heading into a hotel. I followed them. There was a '24 hour' bar and a kind bunch of older ladies, who found my story hilarious and lent me euros for a taxi. I was also handed a pair of shorts and a glass of beer. Things started looking up. I went out and pulled a taxi and just said "Celtic fans pubs." It was a major gamble but it paid off. I started recognising where I was and got dropped off in the early hours just as my friends were getting up to travel. We had hired a car and the drive to Seville was fantastic. We got there and I travelled to the stadium to buy some programs to take home. At this point I could not believe my eyes as there were lots of people holding spare tickets. They were all in the Porto end but I did not care. I negotiated a price of 1500 euros for three tickets. I did not have that kind of cash on me and asked where I could find an ATM. The men who had the tickets pointed to their car and then pointed across the road. They looked really dodgy and I did not want to get in that car. It was a choice between walking away or getting robbed. It was an easy choice in the end because I was still drunk and did not want to miss the game, so I jumped in. We started driving and the guys in the front where chatting in Portuguese. I was shitting myself. They then pointed to an ATM. I requested 1500 euro. The machine rejected me as it was too large an amount. I then tried 100 before it accepted 500. I was again in the middle of nowhere with two guys who did not speak a word of English. I jumped in the back of the car. I said stadium and they put their hand out. I said no money but I will pay at stadium. The men chatted again and then we started driving. The men were arguing and I was close to just jumping out the car and making a run for it. Thankfully we got back to the stadium where my friends were. They had no money on them so I bought one ticket for myself at 500 euros. We then parked the car in a hotel carpark. I travelled to the game alone. When I got there, I saw all the usual Celtic tops everywhere, partying, but there was also another side. I saw people on the street in the scorching heat out for the count, I saw a man who was blind drunk trying to get a "Bust tae Castlemilk." It was quite chaotic at times. I bought a Porto flag to wrap round my Celtic top and went to the match.

After the game there was not a taxi in sight. The only way home was to walk. I had written down the name of the hotel this time to make sure I made it there. When I got there, the car was locked so I went into the hotel for a beer. I was having a great time and started speaking to a Scottish celebrity (don't want to namedrop). She was middle aged and was nothing but nice. I told her of my situation and she said you can maybe sleep on my floor. She said she would be back in a minute and came back with her furious husband who bluntly told me to 'F**k off!' I thanked them anyway and looked outside to see my pals were sleeping in the two seats in the front of the car. They were fully down like the annoying people at the cinema. I just grabbed my beer out the boot and settled down for the night, still upset at the result, in the boot of a Micra! Everything after that was pretty normal.
(Michael Kennedy)

Image courtesy of Vagelis Georgariou

Ever since I was in a London pub just outside of Wembley stadium in 2009, I have enjoyed hearing about the sacrifices that Celtic fans have made. It was at Wembley, that a man with an Edinburgh accent started talking to me. He questioned where I was from, with intrigue. When I told him that I was from Dorset, he said: "Ach so you travel a wee bit to make it up to Parkhead then, ah well that's nothing compared to what my pal's uncle did right. He split with his wife after he went to 'buy a pack of fags' and ended up in Seville… for a month!"

That short bizarre conversation left me wondering how far other fans had gone for Celtic. Here I dedicate a small section to those die hard Hoops.

I was living in Govanhill and at thirteen years of age, was not yet aloud to go to away games. With Celtic playing at Dundee United at the weekend, I told my parents that I had been picked to play for the school team on the Saturday. I directed them not to come as it was an away game and that the team would travel on the school bus. My friends all went along with the story and told my parents the same. Then on Saturday I donned the school football kit and made my way up the road. There I met my friends and we were picked up by a supporter's bus round the corner.

It got rather late and I found out that my uncle reportedly said to Mum: "I bet Colin's gone to Tannadice today, there's no way he got picked for the school team. He can't kick a ball!" When I did finally arrive back home, my friends and I continued the lie and started talking about the phantom school game. It was a 2-0 victory. I thought I'd pulled it off until the Celtic goals were shown on TV later that night. Right after Celtic's first goal, you can see this little lad at the front going mad in his school kit. "COLIN get down here!" Dad yelled.
(Colin Black)

I got the train from Middlesex to Glasgow, just a day after breaking my ankle. Once at Celtic Park, I was told that crutches were not permitted in the Jungle, so I threw them into a bush at the cemetery behind the enclosure and hobbled inside.
(Liam Broad)

In Seville, a Celtic fan jumped into the water fountain and a spike went straight through his groin. Supposedly, the warrior soldiered on and went to the game before collapsing in the second half and being rushed to hospital!
(John Hayter)

Seville sacrifices were aplenty. Thankfully this one was caught on GMTV: a Pakistani-Scot Celtic fan was seen making a phone call to his wife to be, her parents and the fifteen hundred wedding guests in Lahore. He tells them that he won't be able to make the wedding. His stag do in London, with fellow Celtic supporting friends, had led to a detour to Spain instead. "It's once in a lifetime chance. You can get married any day but you can't watch Celtic in a European final for thirty three years. I don't know what the problem is. She'll be ok." He said. His comments were

reinforced by his friends: "The girl has waited twenty years, if she's waited this long then surely another one day in history won't make a difference!" The husband to be, explained that he would make it up to the girl by taking her on a long romantic trip to Monte Carlo. Coincidentally, that was where Celtic would have played the Super Cup, had we won in Seville!
(GMTV scene written about by me)

A couple of years ago I heard the story about a Celtic fan that told his boss that his dad had passed away so that he could get time off for a match. The boss then went round to his house with flowers, only for the supposedly deceased dad to answer the door!
(Brendan McCann)

A friend of mine goes on the Green Brigade site like you and he heard about the sacrifice from a real Celtic dafty on there. His wife would only let him go on one continental trip away each season. But, a number of his mates were going to Copenhagen and he was desperate to go. There was no chance he'd have been permitted to attend another one. However, he was a businessman and flew over Europe regularly. He told his wife, the week before, that he had been called in to a meeting in Germany. She didn't ask any questions, and he secretly booked himself on a flight to Copenhagen with the rest of his mates. His wife dropped him at the airport and he had to go on the trip in his finest suit to make it look real!
(Leanne Whitworth)

I bought my fiancé a lovely engagement ring. Then I came across a ticket for the game in Boavista and I had to sell the ring to get enough money. She ended it but the trip was even better than Seville!
(Andy House)

A good twelve years ago, I lived down South and the only time Celtic was on TV was when we played Rangers. So, when we were playing against Motherwell one midweek night, two friends and I drove four hours up to Liverpool as we had heard that there was a bar that could pick up Scottish football matches on occasion. When we got there, the place was shut! We waited and finally at half time somebody came and opened up for us, having noticed us waiting outside. They managed to get the game on and we drew 0-0. So we drove four hours to Liverpool to see a goalless second half and then immediately drove four hours home for work.
(Josh Bolton)

I hitchhiked from Calderpark Zoo to Madrid in 1980 for the European Cup match.
(Molly)

Celtic played Teplice in the 2003-2004 Season in the UEFA Cup third round and we beat them 3-0 at home, courtesy of two from Larsson and one from Sutton. In the away leg, five of us got a cheap flight to Frankfurt and stayed there overnight with the intention of driving to a hotel in Dresden the next day and driving the remaining twenty six miles to Teplice once we'd checked in and changed. All went well until round about lunchtime on the day of the game when we saw signs for 'Baden Baden' and realised we were driving in the wrong direction and would shortly be in Switzerland! We stopped at the nearest service station and much to the amusement of the watching lorry drivers we had a 'discussion' about why it was we didn't have a map. We then took a vote on our next move (always the democrat!) and decided to bomb it along the autobahn and try to make the game, which was kicking off around 6.30pm, because of the very low temperatures at that time of year. After a fairly hair-raising drive (sorry Eddie!) we arrived at the hotel around 4.30pm. We quickly checked in, donned our specially-bought thermals and asked if we could hire a taxi to take us there and back as none of us could face getting back in the car. For what seemed like buttons, we were provided with a Mercedes minibus with a uniformed driver (who kindly made his first stop at an off-sales) and off we set up the Christmas-card scene that is the mountain pass, which separates Germany from the Czech Republic. The lovely light snowfall seamlessly developed into six feet snow drifts and lorries were jackknifed all over the road. Then, to put the icing on it, we got calls from home and from the stadium to say the game was cancelled due to a power cut. We ploughed on (almost literally); passing first the German border guards and then, about six feet further on, the Czech ones (who kindly ordered us all out of the van, subjected us to some scrutiny and quietly relieved one of our number of £80 he had tucked in his passport holder). By this time the good news arrived that the power was coming back on in the town and the game was likely to be on. We arrived in the town and in a state of near panic we circled the local area (which looked a bit like Easterhouse) asking directions from the women hinging out their windows chatting, and approached the stadium which by then had an ice rink for a concourse. We ran (gingerly) up the stairs and burst through the swing doors on to the stands to see Teplice score the one and only goal of the game! I can say that the pain was relieved by knowing a) that we were through on aggregate and b) that the beer was 50p a pint but it still sticks in my memory as a trip and a half… the things we endure to follow Celtic!

P.S did I mention I was the navigator on that trip?
(Jeanette Findlay – Celtic Trust)

Friendships

From the humble beginnings of Celtic it was inevitable that the Club and supporters would create friendships with fellow clubs throughout the world. Only a few of these friendships have endured and I have chosen to include a selection with genuine history behind them.

Ironically, Celtic had a positive rapport with Oldco Rangers for a short time and also with Hibernian. Both played an integral role in the Club's earliest days and helped us to get a sound footing. However, it was not until the early twentieth century that we developed our first international friendships.

Real Betis:

The story dates back to the foundations of Real Betis and a team named Sevilla Balompié. Sevilla Balompié had been established by a group of students of the Polytechnical School of Seville in 1907. The Club had originally played in blue. However, upon a Spanish merchant's trip to Glasgow in the early 1900s (the exact date is contested), he found himself inspired by the green and white of Celtic. After expressing his admiration, it is thought that Celtic donated their old kit with vertical stripes to the man. He then returned to Seville and ultimately changed the Club's kit and colours. This wasn't just a rash change though. It made perfect sense, with the official colours of the Andalusian flag being both green and white.

A few years later, a group of directors at city rivals FC Sevilla, split from their Club after an internal disagreement. In doing so, they created a new team, which was simply named Betis Balompié. The title of 'Betis' was chosen because it is derived from 'Baetis', the Roman name for the Guadalquivir River which flows through Seville.

The Club initially attracted notable support from the local working class communities, many of whom were Republicans. After establishing itself, Betis took a huge leap forward as they merged with Sevilla Balompié. This amalgamation, which took place in 1914, moulded a club with improved opportunity for success. Interestingly, the name of Betis prevailed in the merger.

Given the nature of the support, it is a little surprising that the Club gained admiration from a number of aristocrats at this time including King Alfonso XIII. Betis then received royal patronage that year and became known as Real Betis Balompié, translating as Royal Betis Football, in English.

The vertical green and white striped jersey is still revered by the Sevillanos as the gift from Celtic. You'll often see Celtic flags dotted around the terraces at Real Betis matches and the Club is now nicknamed the 'Verdiblancos': simply translated as the green and whites.

Belfast Celtic:

In spite of Celtic being a youthful club of the time, the Real Betis relationship was not our only cross border connection. Our very earliest, closest and most important friendship would have to be that with Belfast Celtic. We had toured Belfast in 1889 and drew crowds of over eight thousand to victories against Distillery and United Belfast. It was our first tour and full season and so the crowds for that era were quite staggering.

The Belfast Celts were formed in 1891 and were established in the image of Celtic Football Club in Glasgow. The moulding of the new Club, in its design, extending to include its association with charity, the attractive style of football and an indiscriminate signing policy. The Club Chairman, James Keenan, suggested the name 'Celtic' and Secretary, Bob Hayes, wrote to the Glasgow namesake for their blessing in using the title. Not only did he receive as much, but a sizeable financial donation was also offered in response.

By 1901, the Club became a limited company and had to register as 'Belfast Celtic Ltd' because 'Celtic Football Club Ltd' had already been taken. Their football was played on Donegal Road in West Belfast at a multi-purpose facility named Celtic Park: 'Paradise' to the Belfast Celtic fans! The stadium actually became the first in Ireland to host greyhound racing (in April 1927) and continued to be used as a greyhound track right up until the 1980s.

Belfast Celtic enjoyed very early success, winning the Irish League title in 1899/1900. Their ascendancy and wider symbolism generated big support and they soon became the beacon for the Nationalist community. The Celts had phenomenal ability to draw fans from across the thirty two counties; so much so that special train services were provided for supporters from Dundalk and smaller towns in

County Louth. However, most match goers came from Ulster.

Many people throughout Ireland would follow Belfast Celtic but also the results of their larger namesake in Glasgow. This was reciprocated in Scotland, where an affinity to their County Antrim counterparts was certainly felt. In terms of actual attendance, of course, in that era financial limitation would restrict the ability to travel across the sea on a regular basis.

Savoured it was when the two teams met. On each occasion, the match was held at Celtic Park Belfast, giving the Irish fans a great opportunity to see their beloved teams. Celtic of Glasgow shared the field with the Belfast outfit on no fewer than fifteen occasions, the latter winning just twice. Naturally, huge crowds were lured and gate receipts were often donated to charity.

Results listed below:

1897 Belfast Celtic 0-4 Celtic
1902 Belfast Celtic 0-1 Celtic
1904 Belfast Celtic 1-0 Celtic
1910 Belfast Celtic 0-1 Celtic
1911 Belfast Celtic 0-1 Celtic
1925 Belfast Celtic 0-3 Celtic
1926 Belfast Celtic 2-3 Celtic
1927 Belfast Celtic 4-2 Celtic
1928 Belfast Celtic 0-1 Celtic
1929 Belfast Celtic 4-7 Celtic
1930 Belfast Celtic 1-2 Celtic
1932 Belfast Celtic 0-3 Celtic
1936 Belfast Celtic 1-2 Celtic
1947 Belfast Celtic 4-4 Celtic
1952 Belfast Celtic 2-3 Celtic

One of the key components of the friendship was Charles Patrick Tully. Ireland's original superstar! He was quite a character and a wonderful entertainer. His greatest matches in a Belfast Celtic shirt tended to come against Linfield, and against Oldco Rangers, when wearing Glaswegian hoops. Not only is Tully a legendary link between the two clubs' but he was, as mentioned earlier in the book, the centrepiece behind Glen Daly's 'Celtic Song'. The bulk of the words to Glen Daly's tone are documented in a 1927 Belfast Celtic match programme; further proof that they owned the song first. Tully was a fanatic and brought with him, to Glasgow, the famous anthem.

Tully also brought a wealth of talent and trickery. That talent was nurtured in a typically mischievous manner at St Kevin's School in Belfast. He regularly found himself in trouble for playing what was regarded as a foreign game (soccer) to the premises. Tully skippered the school Gaelic Football team and also played hurling. In spite of his prowess in the Irish codes, it was always association football that he really wanted to play.

Whilst still young, Tully was called up to fill in for a local soccer team at Falls Park. He impressed so much that the legendary Jack Myles came to hear of his ability. Myles was a famous former athlete and then school teacher at Millford Street School. It was renowned for producing footballers. Incredibly, Myles arranged for Tully to be transferred to his institute and sorted him employment as a net boy at Belfast Celtic! Charlie found himself in an environment where he could freely play soccer but still enjoy the game of Gaelic. He won a junior medal in Gaelic Football but his soccer really started to shine.

Belfast Celtic's Coach, Willie MacDonald, had begun to take note of Tully's performances. MacDonald elected to play him against Glentoran in 1942. For once in his life, Tully fell speechless. Jack Vernon, a club legend, had to put Charlie's shirt on and insert his shin guards; such was his shock! Equally shocking was the fact that the occasion marked the first time that he wore shin guards as opposed to stuffing old magazines or newspaper down his socks! He had much more to say on the park and so did the press the next day, who claimed: 'This schoolboy is an outstanding discovery of the future.'

Belfast Celtic sent him out on loan to Ballyclare Comrades and Cliftonville to gain experience. He built on his slender physique and by the mid-1940s he had coveted a regular starting place in the team. It was during this period that his magical playing style earned him the nickname of 'Cheeky Charlie'.

Tully's finest moment in Irish football probably arrived on April 27th 1947, when he scored the winning goal against the team where it all began. That goal against Glentoran handed his beloved Celts the Irish Cup.

Robert Kelly had spotted Tully during a friendly match against Glasgow Celtic a few years prior. He famously said: "Tully would do well here. Our support would appreciate him because he plays the Celtic way." He finally made the move after he had helped the Belfast boys to win the Irish League title in 1948. By contrast, the Scottish outfit had escaped relegation by the skin of their teeth thanks to a hat trick from Jock Weir against Dundee. Some view the desperate situation as the catalyst for the signing.

The deal was sewn up very quickly. Tully said upon joining: "It took me three hours to decide on the Timaloys as opposed to the English glamour clubs, it had always been an ambition of mine to play for the great Scottish Club."

An admired magician on Irish shores, he would cement his place in Glasgow folklore by producing several magic moments throughout a wonderful eleven years at the Club. In 1953 Tully took a corner kick against Falkirk at Brockville. He curled the ball straight into the net, only for the referee to disallow it. Charlie simply retook it and did the exact same again! He had in fact scored direct from a corner on another occasion for Northern Ireland against England. Cheeky Charlie was involved in the memorable Coronation Cup winning side and played in the demolition of Oldco Rangers in the 7-1 League Cup Final of 1957.

If he was loved back home then he was adored in Glasgow. Before long 'Tully cocktails' and 'Tully ice-cream scoops' had arisen in Scottish cafés! Such was the stardom he gained, that he actually began writing a weekly column for 'The Evening Citizen Newspaper' called 'Tullyvision'.

Ironically, he scored against Belfast Celtic in the last meeting between the two clubs'. That particular fixture featured a certain Jock Stein, who was colossal at the heart of the Celtic defence.

In short, Tully is an icon, synonymous with both Celtic editions.

Yet one of the most influential aspects in the relationship was actually the demise of Belfast Celtic. The Club had shattered most Irish records by the outbreak of World War II and looked set to continue in similarly dominant fashion. However, a partitioned Ireland and a changing society would play a key role in post war football.

Belfast Celtic faced Linfield at Windsor Park in December 1948, before a crowd of twenty seven thousand. Linfield largely represented the Unionist community of the North of Ireland. Contests as these were often fiery and this occasion was no different. Linfield finished the match with eight men on the field, Belfast Celtic with ten.

However, it was the brutal actions of the Orange support that would steal the headlines and forever change the future of Irish football.

Belfast Celtic's Jimmy Jones had collided with Jimmy Bryson in the Linfield defence. Bryson sadly broke his ankle on impact. The stadium announcer relayed information to the crowd that Bryson's leg had been broken, further inflaming the local support. The home side actually had another player taken to hospital for severe bruising, which only made the crowd vent more poison.

Amongst mayhem, the Celts were awarded a penalty. Harry Walker scored and the Nationalist's looked set to take the points. The atmosphere turned so sour that many Belfast Celtic fans left early to avoid the predictable trouble. There was no segregation; just a small band of Royal Ulster Constabulary officers.

With only four minutes left, Linfield equalised. Hatred and jubilation combined as the fans spilled on to the pitch. Order was quickly restored and play petered out. Sadly that was not the case at the full time whistle when thousands of Linfield fans ran onto the park and attacked Belfast Celtic players!

Jones was isolated. Given that he had injured Bryson and was a Protestant playing for the 'wrong side', he was made a target. He made way for the running track in a desperate attempt to get up the terracing and shake off his attackers, but they dragged him back down the stairs, laying into him with kicks and punches by the dozen. His life was now in perilous danger!

Linfield supporters jumped and stamped on Jones' leg repeatedly. The police had no control and it was only Sean McCann, Jimmy's close friend and Ballymena goalkeeper, who came to his aide. But the damage had been done and the leg was badly broken. He was rushed to Musgrave Park Hospital, where they managed to save it, though it is now an inch and a half shorter than the other. As a result of the attack the Irish Football Association ordered Linfield FC to play two matches away from Windsor Park stadium.

Belfast Celtic officials called an urgent meeting to discuss the repulsive attack. It is believed that an outcome was agreed but nothing was publicly announced.

After fulfilling the rest of the season's league commitments, the Club embarked upon a tour of the USA. It was extremely successful and saw the Scottish national side (then British champions) famously defeated. However, soon after returning from the glamour excursion, it was announced that Belfast Celtic would withdraw from the Irish League. There was time for one last meeting with Glasgow Celtic in 1952 and a handful of friendly matches; the last being an emotional farewell against Coleraine. After which, the Club completely disbanded.

The significance of this from a Glasgow Celtic point of view was that the overwhelming majority of fans now pledged their sole allegiance to the Scottish Club. Glasgow Celtic was an already established worldwide institution, having won exalted competitions like the Empire Exhibition Cup and had distinguished tours of Europe and the USA themselves. Supporters clubs were formed the length and breadth of Ireland; the first in St Marys (Belfast) in 1952. It was formerly a Belfast Celtic Supporters Club. This transformation made travel to Scotland a touch easier.

As 'The Troubles' kicked off, the Irish based contingent brought with them a hardened Republican mindset into an already politically minded Irish diaspora. The Troubles were very emotive and certainly would have stimulated the political nature of the support and their songbook regardless. Though, the fact that many travelling over were directly affected, intensified and shaped our identity to some degree.

In 2003 the Belfast Celtic Society was formed to resurrect the memory of the Club. In 2010 they immortalised it by opening a museum on the site of the old stadium. Sadly the Celts' former location is now a shopping centre but nevertheless, the museum brings everything to life with a stack full of memorabilia and historical information.

Whilst launching that project, the Society has also created the Belfast Celtic Trail. The route takes you on a journey to pivotal sites in the Club's history. It is largely intertwined with Republicanism and Celtic Football Club alike. The Trail proves popular for many Celtic supporters and is a wonderful way of exploring the connection.

A smaller version of their inspiration, but a huge Club by Irish standards. A grand auld team indeed!

St Pauli:

The void left by the demise of Belfast Celtic has been best filled in the last couple of decades by the supporters of St Pauli in Germany. St Pauli plays sport within the district, in Hamburg. The Club can actually trace its origins as far back as 1862, when St Pauli Turnverein Gymnastics Club was formed. Gymnastics continued as the sole sport at the forefront, almost until the turn of the century. It was then, in 1899, after the Heiligengeistfeld Gymnastics Festival that Franz Reese instigated a sports and recreation department, which would include a football division.

The footballing division did not emerge until 20th November 1906, when members of the Club called for inclusion of the game. The football arm did not begin playing matches or find sufficient numbers to form a team until 1907. It did so with St Pauli TV as its name! Their earliest recorded game was against the footballing wing of a local swimming club (Aegir). The match was drawn one each, and a rematch was arranged, which St Pauli TV romped 7-1.

Only in 1910, was the football side officially established when they registered with the North German Football Association. They started playing in competitive competition in 1911. The team continued to play under the name of St Pauli TV as it reached the top flight for the first time in 1919. The name carried further until, in 1924, they eventually broke from the Gymnastics Club. It was then that the descendant, independent association, namely FC St Pauli came into being. In spite of this, FC St Pauli uses 1910 as their official year of formation. (As an interesting side note, St Pauli Turnverein Club is also still in existence today!)

St Pauli (1910) operated as a traditional sports club. The football dimension, just one part of a larger sporting alliance that plays everything from table tennis to darts! That was until the mid-eighties, when the Club became much more than just a football club. The transformation occurred after a split in the Hamburg support at the time. A rise in hooligan culture across football supports had manifested itself in the form of right wing extremism from some groups on the Hamburg terraces. This didn't sit well with a section of the fans, many of whom would likely have been of a left wing persuasion, this given that St Pauli was traditionally a harbour working class district.

At this time, the government sought to demolish eight houses in the district, which had been the residence of squatters. The community resisted in protest and after a considerable struggle, they were successful in gaining contracts for the squatters to remain.

It was none too surprising then that many people from the St Pauli district felt uncomfortable standing amongst a hardcore of racist support. People broke away from the HSV terraces and went to watch the smaller Club in the city – FC St Pauli. The long left-wing tradition in the district began to influence the supporters of the Club increasingly. St Pauli appeared to become a cult that would take on very much a socialist identity.

Probably, much to the chagrin of the feminists within the support, the Club is based within the heart of the red-light district. That said, the location has actually worked to the Club's advantage in that it has created an alternative fan scene, ultimately based around party atmosphere and left wing politics. In such circumstances, perhaps the greatest achievement is that St Pauli remains a Club for the ordinary working class football fan.

Celtic's friendship with the Club goes back to the nineties when some personal contacts had begun to express the similarities in political views, party attitudes and a mutual respect for one another's support. In a St Pauli fanzine, in 1990, a German author (Dietrich Schulze-Marmeling), who specialises in football matters and in Ireland's unrest; wrote an article on common interests for '*Millerntor Roar!*'. A year later, three members of the fanzine travelled to Britain, where they had arranged to meet with a couple of different fanzine editors. Just a day before the trio's departure, they received a letter from a member of '*Not the View*' Celtic fanzine. The letter had been sent to invite the '*Millerntor Roar!*' editors to Glasgow.

The German's spent two days in the West of Scotland that changed their lives in a very poignant way. Conveniently, Celtic hosted Oldco Rangers at Celtic Park that weekend and the three men were treated to the match, stood in the old Jungle! I quote one of the three, Sven Brux: "It was a mind blowing atmosphere I have never experienced before: the songs, the noise and also the hatred. After the game we were welcomed with incredible hospitality in the pubs around the Gallowgate, where the singing continued. We were caught!" Sven and co reported on their trip to Glasgow in the next edition of their fanzine.

On the back of that article, there were group tours to Celtic's European Cup matches, with further pieces being written. The friendship went from strength to strength and more and more people learned of the connection from either side.

After further opportunities for supporters to mix in Europe, the two clubs finally faced each other in a friendly in 1995. It was FC St Pauli that hosted Celtic, more than repaying the hospitality that we had given them in Scotland. The match brought the curtain down on a tour of North Germany that saw Celtic play a total of four matches. Throughout the tour, St Pauli fans joined the Celtic supporters on their travels to the games. Each time there was widespread partying.

At last the match everyone had been waiting for was upon the large crowds. 'The Irish Brigade' had given the crowd a wonderful intercultural party with all the political, passionate and atmospheric party pieces. A singing competition ensued and the Celtic support belted a powerful rendition of 'The Fields of Athenry', before St Pauli fans joined in. The match itself was poor and uninteresting but the post-match shenanigans more than made up for that. Suffice it to say that punters left the Reeperbahn bars and clubs in the small hours of the morning, in good spirits. It was a fine way for the Celtic support to bid farewell to the St Pauli faithful!

In the years after this trip, Celtic headed to Hamburg to compete against HSV three times. Naturally, the matches drew considerable crowds from St Pauli, who not only wanted to enjoy another party but wanted to voice their opposition at such a bitter rival. These encounters kept the bond alive but it was not until 2010, fifteen years after the initial meeting, that St Pauli would host Celtic again. The match commemorated the centenary of the Club and coupled with a fitting success, which saw them gain promotion to the German Bundesliga.

Due to the eruption of Mount Eyjafjallajökull in Iceland, flight schedules around the globe were drastically altered, leaving many people unable to attend. Nevertheless, those who did make it over seemed to greatly enjoy the amenities and company. There was a fabulous gig in the Jolly Roger pub (main FC St Pauli supporter's pub). On the park, Celtic strolled to a victory by two goals to nil. Paddy McCourt treated the twenty seven thousand people in attendance to the stand out moment with a trademark solo goal. He picked up the ball on the left hand touchline just inside his own half, before he glided past four defenders and curled the ball into the far corner!

In July 2014, whilst Celtic Park hosted the opening ceremony for the Commonwealth Games; the Hoops travelled to face St Pauli once more. This time St Pauli won 1-0 with a confident finish from Nothe in the 38th minute. The match drew a good crowd but slightly fewer numbers than previous encounters…perhaps an indication of the economic climate.

In summary of the friendship, it would be fair to suggest that some social and political parallels initiated contact, but the step to further meetings was almost certainly due to a mutual love of a good party.

The connection ultimately provides the fans of FC St Pauli with the chance to follow a club passionately at European level. For Celtic supporters, the friendship offers the opportunity to experience an 'old school' match day at the football. Gone are the days of standing (soon to return) and beer in Scottish football – the Millerntor gives us the chance to rekindle that, in the name of a Club we admire.

Interview with Sönke Goldbeck (Supervisory board member at FC St Pauli)

Q) What is it about Celtic Football Club that attracted your interest?

A) For quite a while I only had a vague interest in Celtic - I knew that there was some kind of 'connection' and looked at their results with some sympathy, but without knowing much about the Club. It was because of my time in Dublin that I went over to Glasgow for the first time, meeting up with Irish work mates to see a match about 15 years ago. The warm welcome I got from the Celtic support, the growing understanding for the political context, supporting a team in European competitions attracted me in the first place. A lot of beer and a couple of mad parties might have played a role as well.

Q) As a supporter of another club, what do you think that Celtic stands for?

A) I guess we have to differentiate. In the context of how it was founded, it stands for charity, for giving hope and enjoyment to a part of society that is discriminated against both culturally and economically. The implementation of Celtic was an expression of a kind of DIY culture from underdogs of society. Looking at today's Celtic support, these values still play a role. They stand for openness, working class ethics, tolerance, solidarity - and for partying hard without causing too much hassle.

Celtic as the current PLC stands for cold business, decent management decisions, but not that much for the values of the founders, the culture of the Club and the needs of the supporters. It's the supporters, the history and the community that make Celtic, not the PLC.

Q) What do you think is the biggest thing that Celtic and St Pauli have in common?

A) Both were shaped by underdogs and had to use a do-it-yourself approach to get things going. Both are - on average - open towards rather left leaning political ideas. Both are usually willing to stand their ground when attacked, but are rarely attacking others. It's a relatively similar mindset, at least among those that have an actual relationship. It's important to understand, though, that the connection stems from relations between people from both clubs that were more than average engaged in both politics and football. In the end, that's not the majority. Both clubs have idiots amongst their ranks as well and to me it's always about individuals and the relation to these persons. I disdain 'official friendships'.

Q) Finally, you put together a brilliant little magazine for a match between St Pauli and Celtic a couple of years ago. Other than when we play against one another, do you have any dealings with Celtic fans and do you watch Celtic as a second team?

A) I was fortunate enough to forge some strong friendships and make quite a few acquaintances over the years. I communicate with or meet up with those friends often, and social media makes that even easier. As part of St. Pauli CSC, I'm helping with organising our annual St. Pauli - Celtic party and I'm a member of the Millerntor Brigade, our own wee rebel band which had the honour of doing gigs in Glasgow, Dublin, Derry and Belfast among others. Due to a lack of time, I cannot go to Celtic matches as much as I used to, others are going over more often. But I guess I've done about 30 so far, mostly away matches in Scotland and Europe, and yes, I'd consider Celtic my 'second team'. I'm quite critical of the PLC though, and quite fed up with draconian politics against supporters in Scotland.

Villarreal:

Our most recent friendship was formed in the Valencian community in Spain. Indeed the story of our relationship with Villarreal is a quite amazing one. It all begun with a UEFA Cup tie in 2004 when eight thousand Celtic fans travelled to Spain. Typically, a lively atmosphere was enjoyed in the lead up to the match. Despite the support being unrivalled, what really caught the eye of the Villarreal sects was the way that Celtic fans had reacted to defeat. They were so magnanimous and a fantastic party ensued.

The charity of both sets of supporters' played the biggest role in forging the bond. A short while before the tie, son of former Villarreal player, Ernesto Boixader, passed away. There were a number of collections in his honour, which the Celtic support donated to with great generosity.

That is why in January 2005, the Submari Celtic Supporters Club officially opened and had an immediate membership of forty five names. In April of that year, over a hundred Villarreal fans made the trip to Glasgow to visit their friends: something that continued for a further two consecutive seasons. On these trips, supporters came together to raise money for Yorkhill Children's Hospital. The Submari Celtic Club actually outlines charity as one of its three pillars, alongside fun and solidarity.

Charity stays at the heart of the friendship and in 2008 it was massively displayed. The Bhoys faced Villarreal again, this time in the Champions League. Our hosts arranged for both sets of fans to come together in Casel De Festas. By midday the atmosphere was electric as Celtic songs were blasted, drink was flowing and people were wearing mixed yellow and green attire. There were scarfs, t-shirts, pin badges and other merchandise celebrating the connection. Celtic Submari kindly provided paella for the thousands hungry, along with a marching band to enhance the experience. To top the occasion, Neil Lennon paid a visit, where he was given a heroic reception.

Ernesto Boixander, the President of the Celtic Submari Supporter's Club, said: "This has allowed people to make friends, enjoy the game and work together when needed. This is a true lesson to any violent fans." Staggeringly, €15,000, generated through drink sales, merchandise, a raffle and donations, was raised by both sets of fans and donated to the Aspanion charity. The charity supports both children with cancer and their families that need ongoing support. The huge monies made were absolutely incredible for just one day of fundraising and a fabulous exemplification of what these clubs are all about.

Celtic Submari now has over six hundred and fifty members, with one hundred and seventy of those aged under sixteen. They continue to follow our humble beginnings by carrying out charitable activities throughout Spain and for Yorkhill Children's Hospital. To date, the Club has raised over €50,000!

At a more official level, the friendship has taken effect as well. Ahead of the UEFA Champions League match, the Spanish Consul General, Federico Palomera, made a visit to Celtic Park to emphasise the unique bond between the Glasgow Club and Spain. He said: "Spain and Scotland enjoy a great connection and through the positive relationship developed around football, this can only continue. In recent years Celtic Football Club has travelled to Valencia, Villarreal and Barcelona and on each occasion made great friends." Peter Lawwell presented a special Celtic shirt to Federico Palomera, receiving a Villarreal shirt in return.

Officials of both clubs actually came together again in 2014 for a wonderful cause. Villarreal invited Celtic over for a charity match. It had been agreed to allow a thirteen year old cancer patient to play for them and for him to be allowed to score. Young Gohan's dream was made true when he embarked on a weaving dribble and slotted home. The match was in aide of others like Gohan, who suffer from the disease at a young age. Yet again the Hoops fell to a defeat, 4-2 on this occasion. Nonetheless charity was the real winner.

The relationship continues to prosper. Celtic Submari has written a book on the relationship's origins and ongoing successes. Together, we have simply proved an example to football and long may it continue.

Supporter's Groups

Celtic supporters have a unique heritage of forming their own groups. It is a way of taking care of the Club and preserving the interests of fans. The numerous factions each have their own distinctive accounts. The most prevalent of those are recognised here.

Brake Clubs:

The first example of the support organising themselves was with the creation of Brake Clubs. Brake Clubs were mostly restricted to Glasgow and initially consisted of up to twenty five supporters travelling by horse drawn carriage. They would carry a distinct banner, which depicted the Club name and a painting of a Celtic player from the period. The first of its kind was formed in 1889 in St. Mary's parish of the Calton. The original Club's banner proudly bore the name and image of Tom Maley, with the title 'St. Mary's League' at the top. The reference to the 'League' is due to the organisation from which birth was given to the Club - the established branch of the League of the Cross.

The League was actually a temperance society, committed to alcohol abstinence, set up by the Catholic Church. Every parish in Glasgow had a branch of its own. As with St. Mary's, the vast majority of Brake Clubs were also formed in this way. Though, it is quite an oxymoron that within a matter of months, there are references to 'Celtic carriages' being accredited as 'mobile drinking parlours!'

Despite the disobedient charisma, an entire federation of Brake Clubs could soon be boasted. They changed the whole face of football support. In that era, early football fans only tended to attend home matches. However, the wider reach, tendered by horse powered transport, meant that Celtic fans began to pitch up at away fixtures within Glasgow and neighbouring areas. A host of fellowships in the Scottish game followed suit, and the country started to develop a number of active away followings.

As the Brakes became better organised, distant travel became possible and a proper structure was incumbent to have in place. Membership worked in such a way that subscribers would pay a weekly fee, sometimes as high as five shillings. By necessity, payees were viewed as an appendage to the overall continuation of the Clubs. Therefore, value for money was not always at the forefront in leadership psyche. Payment of a stipulated fee entitled a member to travel anywhere. Of course meaning that home games were much less value for money than distant away trips.

Traditionally, the Clubs would congregate in Celtic strongholds. They would then travel together in a large convoy. It must have been quite something to hear the unmistakable pounding of horse shoes on the cobbled streets and see the array of banners – always positioned behind the driver so that they were on display. However, as greater numbers could be accommodated, the tradition of collective club travel fell by the wayside. Only an annual jamboree of the 'United Celtic Brake Clubs' remained.

Members carried a sense of identity, dear. Many were working class, Catholic, Irishmen. Inevitably, the social context that such an aggregation of men found themselves in made them somewhat politically charged. Trade Unionist and Irish Nationalist banners were the norm when on their travels and reported favourites from the songbook were patriotic ballads. 'Wearing of the Green', 'Hail Glorious Saint Patrick' and 'God Save Ireland' were the three widely revered songs that carriage occupants sang. It is also fascinating that after a clash, in which a vehicle was blemished, the perpetrating Oldco Rangers Brake Club, as well as sending four pounds for the damage; said that they would stop singing 'Boyne Water' if their counterparts promised to refrain from singing 'Hail Glorious Saint Patrick'.

Given the Catholic roots of the Brakes, faith played a considerable part in their activity. Some, in 1897, actually called upon Celtic to field an exclusively Catholic team. Most fans were, nevertheless, pleased that this notion was not taken seriously by the football Club. The Catholic and Celtic ethos' of charity was a key motivation for the movement's fundraising efforts. They did a lot of work to raise money on their travels, serving the communities that they represented, beyond reproach.

Yet, for all the culture and commitment, the 1920s saw Brake Clubs enter a fatal decline. The advent of motorised transport and the enhancement of railway lines caused a large loss of membership. People began to travel independently and masses of Celtic supporters enjoyed a match like experience on trains and buses.

Ironically, drunken trouble did little to further the movement's cause. Newspaper articles around the time also allude to complaints of rowdiness, when Clubs' travelled through the night. There was, in fact, strong condemnation from the League of the Cross over the behaviours of some Celtic Brake Clubs; particularly when they collided with fans of Oldco Rangers in Edinburgh. On said occasion, Celtic visited Easter Road, whilst Oldco Rangers visited Tynecastle. The inevitable happened when the two sets of supporters crossed paths. A man (it is undisclosed which team he supported) was thrown from his carriage and struck his head on the neck of one of the horses. The scene was bloody. The clash cemented the erosion of a wonderful tradition, though in reality, the motorised vehicle had signalled the end of the road for horse drawn carriage anyway.

The death of the Brake Club phenomenon did not prevent the circulation of their banners. The banner of the very first 'St. Mary's League' resided in Baird's Bar of the Gallowgate for a number of years until the premises was closed down. It was then auctioned to a collector believed to be living in England, as Celtic Football Club did not make an offer for it!

The nineteenth century banner was not the one with the greatest story behind it though. Instead, that accolade goes to the Sarsfield Celtic Brake Club; hailing from the Gorbals. The Club was named after Patrick Sarsfield, the formidable Irish patriot. Their banner was a material to gloat about, through the story of its tremendous inheritance. It was obtained at some stage during the second decade of the 1900s and was stolen during an altercation with an Orange walk. The Sarsfield group had responded to Orangemen's attempts to march through the Gorbals area. In the clashes, the banner was abducted by an intrepid member. The Lodge graphic was swiftly painted over to display two Celtic favourites. Throughout the years, the emblazoned players have been changed. Upon its last sighting it showed the faces of Joe Dodds and Stevie Chalmers.

An article from the 'Celtic View' in 1968 claims that some people living in the Gorbals could recall the Sarsfield Brake Club leaving Teacher's pub at the corner of Rutherglen Road and Lawmoor Street. They were always led by the Sarsfield Flute Band. It is also rumoured that some Celtic players used to return from away matches on the Club's carriage.

Despite the decline and eventual wipe-out of Brakes, their legacy endures. These were the people that introduced away travel to the game, ultimate dedication, colour and song. The mantle of the Brake Club was carried by a new phenomenon that lives to this day.

Supporters Clubs:
There was a period of transition before the revival of a
supporter's group could come to fruition. Buses,
committees and premises were a prerequisite before the
notion became quantifiable. Eventually, from the ashes of
the Brake Clubs, arose the invention of the Supporters
Club. It was quite the step up in calibre from the exploits of
days gone by. Having taken care of bus hire, leadership,
social convening and bus convening; the first Celtic
Supporters Club, Greenock Shamrock CSC, was founded.
Its remarkable record stretches as far back as 1935.

Like Brake Clubs, the earliest Supporters Clubs paraded
individually styled banners. It was only as they became
main stream, that badges and flags started emerging.

The Celtic Supporters Club allowed people to travel by bus,
in comparable luxury to the days of getting soaked beneath
an inadequate wagon structure. However, the most fantastic
change was the newfound social expeditions. Indeed,
Supporters Clubs became a hub of the community,
enjoying great social enterprise for the first time in the
support's history. No longer were fans invited for tea to
listen to a pianist's gentle tunes. No, now supporters could
hold their own dances, dinners and enjoy a visit from flute
bands.

Supporters Clubs worked together to allow many groups to
acquire premises. The Clubs grew throughout the forties in
Scotland and then in Ireland throughout the fifties. This
allowed supporters from those nations to become more
active in their following of the team. The idea then surfaced
among the Celtic support in England, across Europe and
beyond.

The oldest overseas Supporters Club is Kearney New
Jersey CSC, which was established in 1963. In 2008, The
Bronx Bhoys and New York CSC came together to present

the Club with a 10' x 6' flag, in commemoration of being "The mother overseas and USA Club." Ian Gilmartin, President of Kearny CSC, said in a statement that night: "Nobody will ever come close to having what Celtic Supporters Clubs have. We are a tight knitted family who genuinely care about each other."

Domestic and foreign CSC's alike, enjoy a brilliant social calendar. Many still have bands come to visit or hold trips to events and matches. The beauty of being a CSC member is the comradeship and enjoyment experienced. They also create a small sense of community in the all-encompassing commonality that is the Celtic support. On the one hand, active match attending Clubs allow members to enjoy a song filled ride to games (many of whom make up songs individual to their bus). On the other hand, Clubs from beyond travelling distance can have members gather and bring a sense of the Celtic community to their hometown.

Today, there are close to four hundred Celtic Supporters Clubs in over seventy countries worldwide! Those figures only take into account official registered Clubs and there are in fact over a thousand 'Celtic friendly' bars on the planet.

The measure of the popularity of Celtic Supporters Clubs today, stands in the fact that the largest, Luton CSC, boasts a membership of 1,500 people. The next largest is Lurgan CSC with 800 members. The biggest in Scotland is Dumbarton Harp CSC with over 510 members.

The reach of the clubs are quite astounding. The furthest from Celtic Park are: North - Helsinki CSC (2,057 miles away), South – Melbourne CSC (10,562 ½ miles away), East – New Zealand CSC (11,136 miles away) and West-Waikiki Honolulu CSC (6,892 ¾ miles away)!

For an example of how impactful the CSC idea has proved, see the piece about the Port Glasgow No1 Branch in the characters subdivision of the supporter's stories chapter.

One of the early Celtic Supporters Club buses arrives at the Old Celtic Park – Image donated from Jamie Fox's collection

Supporters Club Associations, Affiliations and Federations:

The power of Celtic Supporters Clubs demanded the formation of a number of bodies and associations. The earliest, founded in 1944, was 'The Celtic Supporters Association'. Then followed 'The Affiliation of Registered Celtic Supporters Clubs', in 1986; 'The Association of Irish Celtic Supporters Clubs', in 1998, and lastly, 'The North American Federation of Celtic Supporters Clubs'.

Celtic Supporters Association:
The Celtic Supporters Association (CSA) was founded by
Willie Fanning in September 1944. Willie was a fervent
Celtic supporter and, like most fans; he had become tired of
the Club's nonchalant approach to war time football. After
seeing his beloved 'Bhoys' demolished 6-2 by Hamilton,
he made the decision to make a long time idea, a reality.

Willie saw the void that the demise of the 'United Celtic
Brake Clubs' had left in terms of a connection between the
support and the Club. It was with that in mind that, soon
after the match, Willie wrote to the 'Daily Record' to
request that fans interested in forming a Supporters Club
contact him. He received a measly fourteen replies. But
undeterred, Willie called an ultimately successful meeting
at the Catholic Parochial Hall in Shettleston. The outcome
was the formation of a committee: Willie Fanning elected
as President. By the time a second meeting was held at the
Ancient Order of Hibernians Hall, in Townhead, the word
of this Club had travelled from mouth to ear throughout
what seemed like half of Glasgow. Publicity was helped, in
no small part, by Mr. Waverley, a respected sports reporter
for the 'Daily Record'. Having witnessed the initial letter
that Fanning published in the paper – he felt sympathy to
the new venture.

The huge and unexpected turnout meant that the meeting
took a different direction, both literally and in regard to the
discussion. The Hall was overflowing, so much so that the
attendees had to defer outside. Instead of discussing the
intended plans moving forward, the committee decided to
work on a new constitution that allowed them to become an
amalgamation of Supporters Clubs and serve as an almost
governing body. That role was given credence, following a
string of meetings conducted from the boxing ring at the
larger Grove Stadium Boxing Arena. Celtic Football Club
officially endorsed the Association, just a year after
establishment. By then, the Association had seven hundred

members under its wing. Celtic handed them the role of distributing tickets to their affiliated branches: an often thankless task as one can imagine. Yet they would surpass early wants, by serving the Club in a practical manner, not least in their suggestion of introducing a dress code for the ball boys at Celtic Park.

Several other clubs contacted Mr. Fanning for assistance in setting up a duplication of the body. No fewer than five supports had been provided with guidance, including the darkest of foes, Oldco Rangers. However, the mark of the Association's influence, closer to Parkhead, showed when Celtic approached them to intervene in a belligerent saga between the legendary Jimmy Delaney, and the Club.

In spite of a healthy relationship with the board, the CSA sought to unchain its official connection and assert themselves as an individual organisation. The bold decision was made, due to the ongoing mediocrity on the field, leading to a set of questions being presented to the board - without adequate response.

In independence, the Association combatted stringent ration practises that had carried over from the war. In the face of restricted food, electricity and travel, the Association managed to transport maimed soldiers from Erskine Hospital to Celtic Park for matches. Such is the mystique of the story; the conscripted servicemen were often taken to hired venues, such as Orange Halls (!), after games. Tea and sandwiches were aplenty in the Halls but the greatest morale boost was in the form of legendary Celtic figures that would pay a visit.

Breaking from the Club also allowed the CSA to acquire twelve branches, not least a Glasgow branch that was so large it could run eleven coaches for different trips. One outing was to the England V Scotland match at Wembley in 1946, which saw the applications being blocked at 650 names! The CSA outlets assembled on Saturday mornings beside George Square, to head for away fixtures.

Apologies flooded to the organisation after they overcame the many doubts, of all but Mr. Waverley, in the journalism world. Their warmth and will to assist older fans was a far cry from the writers' foretelling of "A return to the hooliganism and rowdiness of Brake Clubs!"

The years following have seen an extension in the number of acquired branches to the excess of 130. The remarkable size of the Association has led them to open two social clubs. The best known of the two is situated on London Road, not far from Celtic Park or the Club's former Barrowfield Training Centre. This facility has recently been refurbished and now looks really impressive with huge murals printed on the games room walls. It has become a shrine to Celtic and a superb venue in the social calendar. Speaking of which, the CSA holds an annual Rally that traditionally involves a meal, a band and a guest of honour. The event has been widely regarded as one of the centrepieces of the Celtic year.

Affiliation of Registered Celtic Supporters Clubs:
Similarly, The Affiliation of Registered Celtic Supporters Clubs (ARCSC) was born to serve the interests of the support. However, it is a little more exclusive to the CSC.

The group was founded in 1986, when Eddie McCafferty found himself and many other Supporters Club members unable to obtain match tickets. At this time a lot of Supporters Clubs couldn't gain membership of the CSA either. The dilemma inspired Eddie to contact the 'Celtic View' with a proposal to rectify the problem. A meeting was held in The Broomfield Tavern (Provanmill) between Celtic directors and over three hundred supporters. Eventually, the Celtic board gave official approval for a constitution to be set down. The Affiliation of Registered Celtic Supporters Clubs was now active.

The group would behave in much the same way as the CSA. In no time, it found itself acquiring membership from right across the UK, Ireland, and as far as Canada! Much like Willie Fanning's institution, the ARCSC not only became involved with distribution of match tickets, but it held a number of events to benefit charitable and social needs.

The original constitution is stated below:

1. The organisation will be known as "The Affiliation of Registered Celtic Supporters Clubs"

2. It will be set up to further the aims, ideas and principles of Celtic Football Club.

3. The committee will consist of a Chairman, President, Secretary, Media Officer, Treasurer and Ticket Convenor, voted to office by member clubs at an annual general meeting.

4. Membership will be available to all clubs, registered at Celtic Park for the sum agreed; per club, per season.

5. Membership fees are payable at the start of each new season.

6. The purpose of this body is to promote harmony and co-operation between all member clubs in travel, fundraising, charitable causes and social activities, co-ordinating to take advantage of facilities made available to a larger unit and to get the best possible financial terms in relation to costs, especially travelling to Europe and such like matches.

7.　Regular updates either by meeting or via e-mail so those representatives of each member club can attend to discuss all relevant business. Make decisions and vote on policy matters affecting 'the Affiliation'.

8.　We would ask that every effort is made to ensure that good behaviour and discipline is maintained in all travels when following Celtic Football Club. If indiscretions are committed and are proven, this could possibly affect the allocation of tickets due to the offending, from Celtic Football Club for future matches. Everything possible will be done at all times to ensure the good name of Celtic Football Club and to enhance the reputation of Celtic supporters throughout the football world.

The ARCSC became an important group, championing the name of the Club and all that encompasses it. The body is almost a social organisation that assists member clubs in all manners possible. Since inception, The Affiliation has taken coaches to Celtic themed plays, dances and productions. It is littered with engagement in popular (Celtic) culture.

Charity has scarcely been apart from the organisation. From incalculable events like a climb of Ben Nevis to Christmas appeals - the Affiliation finally embodied charity through an event of their own. Since 2007, on an annual basis, it stages its own five-aside tournament in aide of the local needy.

Association of Irish Celtic Supporters:
The creation of The Association of Irish Celtic Supporters Clubs (AICSC) or Cumann Tachaíocta Ceilteach Gaolach was very different. The organisation emanated towards the end of Wim Jansen's only season in charge of the Club. A fanatical Celtic support on the Emerald Isle had been heightened with the buzz that the McCann era generated.

But, in the view of many, Fergus McCann's 'Bhoys Against Bigotry' campaign was an attack on the Irish identity of the Club and an outright attempt to dilute it. Against this backdrop, the first AICSC meeting was held in Monaghan. The topic of the Club's identity was discussed and it was decided to pool together the resources of all Supporters Clubs, to gather a communal voice. The following objectives were outlined in writing:

A) To organise and unite the existing Celtic Supporters Clubs in Ireland and to encourage and promote the formation of new clubs within the boundaries of Ireland. It will also be a non-profit, non-political and non-sectarian organisation.

B) The Association shall also seek to preserve and strengthen the links that exist between Celtic F.C. and Ireland

C) The Association affirms its support for Celtic's Social Charter and the Celtic Football Club Mission Statement

The Association now rotates meetings on a province by province basis to make them more accessible for each Supporters Club around the country.

Subsequent to the desire for an official voice to represent Irish Celtic fans, the Association capitalised on its position and produced 'The view from the 32' magazine.

The committee diversified from its initial commitments, to also arrange several inexpensive trips to away matches throughout Europe. This is perhaps the most commendable trait of the organisation. But it didn't stop there and in the last few years the organisation has been able to introduce a broad range of merchandise.

The undoubted highlight of the AICSC year is an annual dinner event held in Dublin. The first such occasion was visited by a whole host of Celtic legends including Sean Fallon, who later became Honorary President. Each dinner since, has seen Club greats involved. Celtic fully endorses the event and joins in the wonderful celebration of the Irish connection. Unsurprisingly, the meal is attended in overwhelming numbers. The most recent dinner event granted a particularly upholding occasion when everybody rose to their feet and gave a huge round of applause to young Irishman, Jay Beatty. Jay, suited and booted, proudly stood on a chair by the microphone and introduced himself by shouting: "UP THE HOOPS!" It was a typically impassioned shout from the youngster and he continued, leading the guests in a proclaiming of "Here We Go Ten in a Row."

North American Federation of Celtic Supporters Clubs:
Representative of a quite different region, The North American Federation of Celtic Supporters Clubs was the latest of supporter's bodies to come into existence. There is not a clear date as to when the organisation was officially founded. However, we do know that it was brought into place to serve as an umbrella organisation for the CSC's in the USA and Canada.

The Federation does a quite remarkable job to bind together groups of supporters across such a vast area and differing time zones. They achieve this by having representatives of both the East and West coasts. The Federation also attracts membership from South America and a handful of clubs across the world. Even in the UK, some CSC's have enlisted with the body. As ever, The Federation endeavours to assist those groups in whatever manner possible.

The organisation's crest is the four leaf clover, with the national flags of the USA, Canada, Ireland and Scotland depicted upon each leaf. It is predominantly supporters from those countries that they benefit each year, in the largest event on the calendar. This is because the Federation holds a Celtic Convention in the USA at the end of the season. Vegas is the chosen venue every other year, and the conventions between are rotated around the region. The Federation does great work in organising a suitable location and helping overseas supporters, through partnering with travel agents. Year on year the event improves.

The first Las Vegas Celtic Convention attracted a couple of thousand Hoops! The amenities were phenomenal and Celts like Niall McGinn took the opportunity to soak up the sun at the event.

At time of writing, the 2015 Convention is upon us. The event looks to be the pinnacle of all so far. There is a great itinerary including: a pool party, cabaret night and a golf day. That trio is in combination with Paul Larkin's 'Asterisk Years', live music from Paddy Ryan's band, a dinner dance, broadcasting of the Ireland v Scotland European Qualifier and a Celtic inspired farewell pub night. The craic doesn't need explaining but, in the interests of accuracy, I confirm that alcohol is absorbed keenly. As is the cracking climate and a great few days is always had by all. Additionally, this year there will be considerable sums raised for the Kano Foundation.

Celts For Change:
Formed in September 1993, after the 'Save Our Celts' group's demise; 'Celts For Change' battled to oust the old board and seek a brighter future for the football Club. Their initial committee comprised of five key men: Matt McGlone, who was the face of the organisation and at the time, editor of 'Once a Tim' fanzine; Brendan Sweeney, Colin Duncan, David Cunningham and John Thompson.

The group's predecessor, 'Save Our Celts', had served as a good example to the committee. 'Save Our Celts' was founded by Willie Wilson in 1991. They held an opening meeting with an attendance of just over three hundred, and further rallies/meetings attracting more. A host of high profile speakers such as overthrown board member, Brian Dempsey, and Lisbon Lion, Jim Craig got involved. Despite its early success, an ever decreasing morale among the support led to an irreversible decline.

Willie Wilson was invited to join 'Celts For Change' but decided not to do so. However, it was he who pointed Brendan Sweeney in the direction of the group. Having learned from the previous effort, 'Celts For Change' aimed to present the frustrations of the support as one. These frustrations would be of relevance to the overhaul of the board and ultimately the removal of the practice that was coined the 'biscuit tin' (lack of spending).

The group set about their aims with quite radical action, something that caught the attention of the media and bolstered efforts immensely. A protest outside the Royal Bank of Scotland was perhaps the first real poignant breakthrough in terms of press coverage. Consequentially, the Celtic support started to recognise 'Celts For Change' as the group to champion their concerns and bring about genuine transformation.

Matt McGlone's influence at 'Once a Tim' fanzine ensured that flow of information was maintained and the exposure given to their 'back the team, sack the board' mantra, seemed to generate an unstoppable momentum. By the time BBC News gave coverage to a scene from 'Celts For Change' Rally, meetings at City Halls were being filled to the brim.

With that said, the organisers didn't operate without opposition. These days there seems to have been some revisionism that suggests the entire support hated the old board and wanted the see the back of them. There was in fact a quite clamorous minority that felt differently. Thankfully they remained little more than that, but none the less they were an element that needed curtailed.

The committee and its members worked with a relentless enthusiasm, but their finest hour will always be noted as 1st March 1994. The group had organised an official boycott of the rearranged home match against Kilmarnock. Small sections of the support chose not to give up their enjoyment of watching Celtic, whilst some others felt that a boycott strayed from the ideal 'back the team, sack the board'. Although most trusted the group's guidance.

Celtic beat Kilmarnock by a goal to nil. Yet hindsight shows that the post-match attendance figures were of more importance. The official Club attendance was given as 10,055. Little did they know that 'Celts For Change' had employed an outside agency to stand at the turnstyles and count the genuine attendance on the night. Their figure: 8,225. The key here is that the break-even requirement stood at ten thousand paying fans. Therefore, the boycott was a success.

A matter of three days passed before the exposing that 'Celts For Change' had created, led to the last minute takeover of Celtic Football Club by Fergus McCann. Just a day earlier, on 3rd March 1994, the board had called a press conference, which they claimed would be "The most momentous in Celtic's history." The conference consisted of plans for a Celtic village in Cambuslang and the willing financial backing of the project from a Swiss Bank. These astonishing claims were found untrue and the reputation of the board plummeted to horrendous levels. Less than twenty four hours later, Brian Dempsey emerged at the steps outside Celtic Park. It was then that he proclaimed his immortal words: "The battle is over. The rebels have won!"

It was a great victory for the so called 'rebel shareholders' that were Fergus McCann and Brian Dempsey, among others. Per contra, the role that 'Celts For Change' and its organisers played in this success should not be understated. It was every bit a victory for them and the Celtic fans that played their part.

Soon after the takeover, the group ceased to exist. Matt McGlone was offered a role with 'Celtic View' magazine; he is now editor at the impressive 'Alternative View' fanzine and is held in high esteem. Brendan Sweeney joined 'Celtic Graves Society' and both he and McGlone, had conjoined to form 'The Jungle Bhoys' before their latest endeavours. The other members returned to relative normality. That is not to say that they should be forgotten.

Each of committee are legends, who took action and won. Their efforts are recognised in stone outside of Celtic Park, where the Club positions a plaque in tribute to the group. At its unveiling, Brendan Sweeney commented: "We weren't there to tell the fans what to do. We were there to do what the fans wanted us to do, we were representing them. We were five working-class guys from the Jungle, with all different opinions, but we all shared the same bond. It's fantastic to have this plaque. For me it signifies the people at the Club and how in touch they are with the Celtic supporters. For twenty years we've seen a lot of people come and go but the support is the one thing that remains constant."

Celtic Trust:
In 1999, The Celtic Trust was established in order to represent small shareholders within Celtic PLC. Its aim is to give ordinary fans a greater say in the running of the Club. Yet it is far from limited to this ambition. The Trust has in fact been conscious of the local community and like Celtic Football Club, has aimed to serve it where possible. This very core of The Trust was exemplified in 2005, when

after a long running campaign, with which The Trust was well represented; a statue of Brother Walfrid was erected outside the main entrance to Celtic Park. The shrine to our main founding member reminds one and all of the social and cultural ethos of this great Club.

Different factions of the Celtic support have also been known to approach The Trust concerning a wide range of issues, from ticket pricing to the treatment of our fans. To their credit, The Celtic Trust has worked tremendously hard on these issues and has achieved some great victories.

At the time of writing, Celtic supporters worldwide are celebrating the news that safe standing has been given the go ahead for the start of the 2016/2017 season. It was The Celtic Trust that played a leading role from the initiation of the plans and they, together with other supporter's groups, have collaborated with the Club to secure this most popular achievement. The Trust is also combatting another serious problem at present – The Offensive Behaviour at Football and Threatening Communications (Scotland) Act 2012.

The Act, a complete scandal as shown by lack of conviction rates, has been viewed by many as an attempt to sanitise Scottish football. Not long prior to this heinous legislation, Fans Against Criminalisation (FAC) group was set up, with The Celtic Trust among five bodies coming together to create it. Their position gained significance when the SNP rushed the Bill through parliament and began targeting football fans. Since, FAC have campaigned for the abolition of the Act and have helped to fund legal proceedings for supporters. Their action has taken many forms but was put in the public eye with demonstrations at George Square.

The current Celtic Trust committee is made up of twelve dedicated Celtic fans from differing backgrounds. They were elected in to their position by way of a democratic vote at the organisation's AGM. One of three trustees, Jeanette Findlay, kindly offered to speak with me regarding her role within the organisation.

Interview with Jeanette Findlay

Q) Firstly, could you tell readers a little bit about the Trust and your role within the organisation?

A) The Celtic Trust is an Industrial and Provident Society which is regulated by the Financial Conduct Authority. It is set up like that because we own shares and seek to own more so that ultimately (maybe not next year!) we (ie its members at the time) would take ownership of Celtic. That is the long-term aim of the Trust, for Celtic to be owned and controlled by the supporters. In the meantime we intervene annually in the PLC AGM and the rest of the year we act like (and in cooperation with) other supporters' organisations to represent our members and seek to make things better generally for the fans. I was one of the founder members and was Chair for a number of years. I am no longer the Chair but I remain on the Trustee Board.

Q) What would you say has been the greatest thing that you've been involved in with the Celtic Trust?

A) Setting the Trust up as the correct legal and financial vehicle for owning Celtic was a mammoth task (it took nearly two years) but that is like groundwork – vitally important but not seen once you start building. Our campaign around the Living Wage is probably the most important thing we are doing now but we have been involved in a number of things e.g. building the Walfrid Statue, getting a Dividend Reinvestment Scheme in place to spread share ownership, putting forward the idea of an annual charity match among others. What people don't see though and what I take a great deal of pride in, is our work representing individuals who have come into conflict with the Club and helping to sort out those issues. To use another analogy, we are a bit like trades union reps covering personal cases. Our Secretary, Marie McCusker, puts an enormous amount of time into that, as do others. No-one hears about it but it is vitally important to the people involved.

Q) I know that you've been involved with FAC and have worked hard to oppose the OBAF Bill. Though far from being an organisation that is exclusive to the Celtic support, could you tell us how some of the issues you've been tackling, have affected Celtic fans?

A) Our work with FAC is very time-consuming and has taken up a large chunk of my time over the past three years. Although it was set up by the five main Celtic supporters' organisations, it was never intended to be just about Celtic supporters. We have in fact offered support, financial and moral, to supporters of Hamilton, Motherwell, Hibs and Rangers and we continue to offer support to any football supporter caught up in this pernicious legislation. However, it would be fair to say that Celtic supporters are more likely to contact us to seek help. There are very particular issues regarding the Act which affect Celtic supporters although it is a bad thing for all supporters. The Act itself was, in my view, brought in to criminalise Celtic fans because all of the other behaviours that it ostensibly covers were already covered by existing legislation. What wasn't covered was the expression of support (songs, flags, t-shirts) etc for political causes, chiefly around Irish unity and independence. It is hard to credit, but we spend most, though not all, of our time on issues arising from one particular song, 'The Roll of Honour'. It is simply not acceptable that we can have young, otherwise law-abiding citizens, criminalised for singing a song – actually any song but definitely not a song which arises from their ethnic and political identity. This is not a debate about whether such songs should be sung at football matches and there are clearly a variety of views around that. It is about whether if you take one particular view, you should be subjected to prosecution. So really the issue for Celtic fans has been about saying our civil and political rights and rights to freedom of expression cannot be denied simply because of where we happen to be or where we are in transit to or from. The impact of this Act on all supporters, including Celtic supporters has been enormous. The cost of the harassment and victimisation of fans is also enormous and maybe that is what will ultimately be its downfall rather than any issue of principal. We shall see.

Q) To hold such positions in the Celtic community you must all have a real passion for the Club and its supporters. What does the Club mean to Trustees?

A) Celtic is an enormous part of our lives, although I would have to say that I would prefer it to be more about going to the games and enjoying myself than it currently is, largely because of the battles around the Act! I would make the distinction here between Celtic as a community and Celtic PLC. Celtic PLC means nothing to me and, as I have said, we look forward to a day when the Club is owned and run by the supporters and not as a private company. Celtic as a community is where I organise, debate, take part in charitable work, political work, express my national identity and, of course, where I socialise and engage with my family and friends. It is peopled by those I love, respect, admire, enjoy their company, their writing, their chat, their enthusiasm, their generosity, their kindness, their solidarity, their wit, their knowledge and their passion. Those who know me will have heard me say this many times: Celtic is the national side of an immigrant people and, it is in this sense, that it is truly, in that often misused phrase, more than a club.

Green Brigade Ultras:
The story of the 'Green Brigade Ultras' could fill a book in its own right. To keep this summary of the group organised, I have arranged the section into smaller subdivisions on each component.

A fanatical supporters group called 'The Jungle Bhoys' actually played a lead role in the inspiration of the 'Green Brigade'. It is there that I shall begin.

Jungle Bhoys:
The change to all seated stadia heavily impacted upon the atmosphere at every football ground in the UK but especially at Celtic Park. Without a doubt the big game occasions still conjured an unrivalled atmosphere but less exciting matches started to become drab in the stands at home matches. To counter the issue, Matt McGlone and Brendan Sweeney (with the help of others) brought 'The Jungle Bhoys' to existence in 2005.

Seated at times in the North Stand Upper tier and at others in the Jock Stein Stand Lower tier, the group put together some unbelievable displays, particularly on European nights. The famous 'Welcome to Paradise' flag display and tri-colour display for the matches against Spartak Moscow and Barcelona were headline efforts. To gain the necessary funding for these displays, the group had to sell programs and plead for donations on their forum site. The generosity of the Celtic support was crucial to their development and the group repaid them by becoming the lead section for atmosphere and colour at home matches. Though times with 'The Jungle Bhoys' were enjoyable, some members grew frustrated. Firstly, the group held an a-political stance. They also strongly deflected any suggestions of them being an ultras group and they tended to work closely with the Club; whereas some members wanted them to be a little more independent.

Formation:

In the summer of 2006, the hardcore contingent of 'The Jungle Bhoys' decided that they wanted something a little more impactful and distinct. These people met in Glasgow pubs and discussed the issues that the Celtic support faced. They looked at the way in which fans supported their team on the continent, the political leanings of Celtic and the best way to return the Celtic support to one of the very best in the world. Therefore, they decided to form the 'Green Brigade Ultras' and amicably break away from 'The Jungle Bhoys'. The group held an unashamedly political stance, as anti-fascists interested in left wing politics and Irish Republicanism. In addition, they wanted to stand at the football, add colour, atmosphere and connect with the Club's charitable roots.

A banner bearing a skull with a scarf round the neck symbolised the group and the birth of it.

Growth:

In the earliest days, the dozen or so members would congregate in section 111 of the North curve at Celtic Park. They'd sing together and activate those around them, before the section became identifiable as the place to head to if you wanted an atmosphere. Cup matches gave the group a great opportunity to test their ability, as less season ticket holders occupied the seats around the curve. It was then that greater numbers would flock to the section and the novelty that the 'Green Brigade' enjoyed was terrific.

However, the group proved to be much more than a mere novelty. Their membership expanded sharply and people were relocating to that area of the ground on a permanent basis. The 'Green Brigade' had gone from being a very much underground group to an established influence that would produce higher quality banners with every passing match. Indeed, the early days saw banners such as this one:

Green Brigade Easter Lilly banner 2007

Efforts like the above aren't to be mocked but can be reflected upon to show just how far the group have come. It was also around this time that the group started producing merchandise such as ultras t-shirts for members and latterly as a means of raising money through wider sales.

Another faculty of the group in those cradle days was the ability to create songs and integrate them in to the Celtic repertoire. Songs like 'Mo Mo Massimo Donati' ended up being belted by the Celtic faithful, helped when he duly saved the day with a last gasp winner against Shaktar Donetsk. The new songs were an energising cult in the stands, giving the group a good platform from which to build. In no time songs like 'C'mon You Boys in Green', 'The Heat of Lisbon', 'Just Can't Get Enough' and 'Let's All Do the Huddle' were being created by the group and sang en masse.

The 'Green Brigade' found itself in an established position against the predictions of doubters… of which there were many. This position led to a real improvement in professionalism, particularly in terms of the merchandise and displays produced.

The whole culture surrounding the group captivated the interest of some supporters that had strayed from Parkhead. Once attendances and atmosphere improved to such an extent that hundreds of people were going tonto every second week; it was only a matter of time before the Club officially handed them section 111. This proposition was finally sanctioned in 2010. The ticketing of the section is governed to an extent by the group, whereby they can ensure that all members have a seat and new members can get a season book for the section. Obtaining the section made a real difference. It was from that point that we saw the group kick on and reach unforeseen heights.

A corteo was arranged by the group for members and like-minded fans to walk together from the Brazen Head Pub to Hampden Park for a Youth Cup Final against our now defunct rivals. The corteo brought a healthy crowd that marched, waving flags and reeling off songs that continued inside the stadium. It was the first of a few, each growing in size.

A Green Brigade streamer Display at Ibrox in 2009

The first Corteo in 2010 - walking to Hampden

Charity & Community:
Charity and social inclusion plays as big a role in the
'Green Brigade' as it does at the Club itself. To their
absolute credit, the 'Green Brigade' has carried out an
immense amount of work to benefit the less fortunate. For
the last seven years the group has hosted an Annual Anti-
Discrimination Tournament. The competition has gone
from a small football tournament to a community event that
is a constitutive part of the season's calendar. The event
aims to challenge intolerances, in the spirit of Celtic,
through the mediums of football, beer and fun. Over the
years, teams from marginalised communities have been
invited to partake, pitting their wits in small sided matches
against a host of teams assembled in the Celtic community.
It is quite an inspiration to see Glaswegians mistime tackles
against African immigrants and such like. The order of the
day usually involves some entertainment for younger
guests; awful football, a barbeque and a good drink fuelled
sing song. Celtic has always been a Club that is open to all,
a policy embodied by the support, and the non-discriminate
nature of the group really reflects well.

The 'Green Brigade' Ultras also serve the community on a more regular basis. At the local level, they run regular paint nights. These give people a chance to have a social meeting in a relaxed setting. Furthermore, the group hosts education nights, where typically a world issue or political topic is discussed. A guest speaker(s) is/are invited to present their knowledge on a chosen subject before a question and answers session concludes proceedings. Political education ranges from a stringent struggle of the Iraqi people to the ins and outs of an independent Scotland. The greatest achievement of the talks is that they have captured the imagination of the youth and have inspired a new generation of people to become politically active.

The 'Green Brigade' is a member of the Alerta Network and Antifa Movement. They take proactive measures in everything from local to global affairs. Like many Celtic supporters, multiple members attend Irish Republican parades, commemorations and marches. Interestingly, members can also be found at Palestinian freedom demos, anti-militarism protests, and socialist activism events. Their belief in justice and the manner in which they enthuse about politics has gripped a small section of the support.

The group take their politics far more seriously than most Celtic fans but they can be said to have widened the scope of sympathies to causes other than, yet similar to, Irish Republicanism. A reigniting of visible support for the International Brigades, the Palestinians, the Basques and the Catalonians pay tribute to that.

A Palestine Flag given pride of place v Inverness 2015

The latest political campaign sees the group launch its very own 'Bethlethem2Belfast' project. If successful, youth footballers from Aida and Deheishe refugee camps in Bethlehem, Palestine, will be able to play football in this year's annual Anti-Racism World Cup in Belfast. Transporting people form one part of the world to another is simple under normal circumstances. However, the refugee camps mentioned, come under regular attack from Israeli occupying forces. Therefore, the depth of feeling against the Israeli's in these camps, mean that an already oppressive regime becomes more so, when it comes to granting visas.

The plan for 'Bethlehem2Belfast' is for the 'Green Brigade' to raise awareness and get enough Celtic Supporters Clubs to sponsor each player so that pressure is mounted on Israel to grant the visas required. Sponsorship money will see that flights and accommodation costs are covered. If the project succeeds it will give these children a welcome relief from the brutalities back home. They will be entered into an unusually safe environment, where they will be surrounded by solidarity and care.

In terms of direct charitable action, the 'Green Brigade' has also been excellent. Over the years they have held a lot of fundraisers with a wealth of beneficiaries. Their most recent charity night was actually attended by Ronny Deila. That is a mark of just how well known and received the group and their charity nights have become. Be that as it may, the closest aligned action of the group to the founders of Celtic has been the food banks that they have arranged.

It is sad that in this day and age people in Glasgow still go hungry. Nevertheless, the 'Green Brigade' first held an official food bank two years ago. A year after that, they held another, which overwhelming broke the UK record – five tonnes of food were donated by the classy Celtic support!

On April 15th 2015, twelve organisations including Celtic FC Foundation, Green Brigade, CSA, Celtic Trust and Celtic Graves Society etc. decided to mark the anniversary of Brother Walfrid's passing. Brother Walfrid actually passed away on April 17th but as Celtic hosted Kilmarnock two days sooner, a large foodbank collection named 'Walfrid's Legacy' was arranged in his honour. Walfrid passed away one hundred years prior but how he must have been proud looking down on his team's supporters that night. Extraordinarily, the collection broke UK records again! The overwhelming achievement was reached due to the donations of seven and a half tonnes of food, plus additional nine thousand pounds cash.

High points:
Knowing that there are far too many high points to mention, I decided to run a little survey when I was in the Gallowgate last year. I asked punters from Chrystal Bells, The Saracen Head, Hoops Bar and Bar 67, their thoughts on the group's finest moments. Five highs ranked above the rest and are listed in order.

5) The 'Green Brigade' had somebody infiltrate the ranks of 'Blue Order' (Oldco Rangers ultras group) a few weeks before the derby match in December 2008. The 'agent' collated information of a planned banner and returned his findings to the group. At half time in the derby, with the score goalless, the 'Blue Order' finally unveiled their display. It was an image of a bus that slandered Celtic with a few insults written. Hilariously, the 'Green Brigade' unveiled a counter banner bearing a quite different bus and some fabulous mockery of their own. It left the 'Blue Order' red faced and one fan was jaw dropped – quite literally. Laughter spread across the Broomloan Road Stand, whilst the initial banner was frantically removed. A cameraman managed to capture the scene with two wonderful photos. One, of the Green Brigade's response, and another of an open mouthed Oldco Rangers fan, stood beside his original effort.

Images of the original banner and response were not permitted for print. To view them, I urge you to search online for 'Green Brigade bus-ted display'. You will then find and enjoy both!

4) Next, punters ranked Neil Lennon's gesture of dedicating the SPL trophy to the group at number four. To gain the appreciation of the manager is a fantastic complement to the 'Green Brigade'. Perhaps this recognition came from the previous season when Lennon had overwhelming personal difficulties. At that time, having had genuine threats to his life, the 'Green Brigade' produced an array of banners giving him much needed support. A year later, Lennon had masterminded Celtic to the title. After defeating Hearts 5-0 in the last match of the season, the boss walked to the corner flag in front of section 111. Once there, he saluted the 'Green Brigade' and left the trophy in front of them. Speaking to the press that evening Lennon said: "I just wanted to say thank you to them because they have, week in, week out, created a great atmosphere. They sing non-stop. They add colour. Sometimes they are a little bit controversial but in the main they have behaved themselves impeccably and they have changed the culture of the stadium. It's a fun place to come for the supporters and the atmosphere in the big games has been fantastic. They are the catalyst for all of that."

3) At third, is the immortal 'Scotland's shame' banner. When discussing its unveiling, almost everybody smiled. I am told that the banner was a year in the planning and climbed from the back burner when the appropriate opportunity arrived in April 2008. Just as now, Rangers, in their previous incarnation, were very unpopular in 'Paradise'. In fact the behaviour and bigotry of 'the people' could often be described as shameful. So at half time, a goal to the good in a crucial derby; the 'Green Brigade' displayed their elusive banner. It read 'Scotland's Shame' with an arrow pointing to the Oldco Rangers fans. It was passed along the tier and worked its way right beside the away section.

Scotland's Shame Banner 2008

2) I cannot fail to include the four horsemen banner in this subdivision. In 2012, Oldco Rangers were in administration, destined for death. A packed away section at Celtic Park, in the final ever derby match, attempted to gloss over things with a show of defiance. Thanks to the 'Green Brigade', they had no chance of hiding their fatal eventuality. With the stadium full before kick-off, area 111 unveiled one of the most intellectual and effective displays you are ever likely to see. A huge banner draped from the upper tier, showing the four horses of the apocalypse, ridden by none other than: Neil Lennon, Craig Whyte, Hector the Taxman and Armageddon! A compounding caption read: 'Your day is coming.' On the artwork surrounds, were several tombstones inscribed with belittling phrases such as: 'you'll not be missed.' As this magnificent tifo was revealed, 'Paradise' stood still. The moment captures the Celtic mentality wonderfully: sharp witted and creative. It was a fine way to bow out of the rivalry on top.

Four Horsemen of the Apocalypse – Image courtesy of Jamie Fox

1) Following the accurate forecast of Oldco Rangers' death, Celtic and the support went from strength to strength. In November 2012, the Club celebrated its 125th birthday. The 'Green Brigade' ensured that the landmark would be marked colourfully. When the teams left the sanctuary of the tunnel and stepped into the cauldron that was Celtic Park on a European night; they were greeted by the best show of colour that Celtic has ever boasted. In huge emboldened font, across from them in the towering North Stand, a message reading '125 Celtic' was displayed against a green and white hooped background. At the Jock Stein Stand, supporters exhibited a red Celtic cross, while the Lisbon Lions Stand bore a more conventional green cross. The Main Stand completed the scene with a throng of hoops.

Thankfully, the display inspired both the players and the fans, who gave everything in equal measure. The combined efforts led us to one of the greatest results in the Club's lifetime. The unprecedented creativity of the 'Green Brigade' was showcased to the world of football. Extensive credit must go to the group for not just planning the display, but fundraising to ensure the idea would become reality. The generosity of the wider support, to offer funds and lend a helping hand in setting up materials was also incredible.

Green Brigade full stadium display

Controversy:
Throughout the ups and downs, the 'Green Brigade' has sailed close to the wind. Their fondness for the use of pyrotechnics has landed both themselves and the Club in trouble with the authorities before. Yet it is probably their hardened political beliefs and unashamed expression of those that has proved most controversial.

The group has held a strong stance over the poppy debate. They displayed a hugely divisive banner at Celtic Park in November 2010 reading: 'Your deeds would shame all the devils in hell, Ireland Iraq Afghanistan, no bloodstained poppy on our hoops'. The banner left no doubt as to the feeling of members in regards to Celtic Football Club deciding to embroider the shirt with a poppy for Remembrance Day. The banner divided the support with most people viewing it as an improper platform to air the view. Media across the world picked up on it and the group hit international headlines. There was overwhelming condemnation from authorities and establishments and the Club was handed a fine.

Undeterred, the 'Green Brigade' held an official boycott of the following match away at St Mirren. They cited the deaths caused by British forces as the reasoning behind the boycott. In particular, they highlighted 'Bloody Sunday', when the Royal Paratroop Regiment shot fourteen unarmed civilians dead, in Derry, in 1972. Some members have personally told me that the group would be happy to commemorate those that fought in the world wars but that they will not stand for the commemoration of illegal conflicts conducted by the British.

There have been other controversies, including a simple and succinct banner saying: 'F**k UEFA' - a response to the body viewing some of our songs as "Illicit." However, the biggest controversy in UEFA competition was the display that the 'Green Brigade' promulgated in the

Champions League against AC Milan. The match fell at a time when Celtic fans and the group, in particular, had come in for some harsh treatment by the Police. In typical Green Brigade fashion, they showed a public display with no mincing of their words: 'The terrorist or the dreamer, the savage or the brave, depends whose vote your trying to catch, or whose face your trying to save'. There were images of William Wallace and Bobby Sands shown as well. The aim of the display was to highlight the hypocrisy in punishing people for singing Irish rebel songs, whilst promoting Scottish ones. Unsurprisingly, the media didn't like this comparison and UEFA hit Celtic with another fine. For that reason, many Celtic supporters also felt negatively towards the display.

Controversial displays

Criminalisation and being banned from Celtic Park:
Like most ultras, the 'Green Brigade' can be said to have
experienced some harassment from the authorities.
Members have endured searches and materials being
confiscated, which must lead to an uncomfortable match
day experience. Of course that is completely wrong but it's
not something too far from what ultras across the globe
have to put up with.

However, in 2012, many members' lives were turned
upside down. The SNP had hastily passed legislation that
handed police the power to incriminate football supporters,
if they deemed them to be acting in an offensive manner.
The goal of the Bill is supposedly to eradicate sectarianism,
though many Celtic fans beg to differ. Instead, it may
appear more plausible to say that the Bill is an attempt to
even the score between ourselves and our rancid
neighbours. There is no mileage to incriminating Celtic
fans for songs of Irish rebellion because they are not
sectarian and such claims do not stand up in court.
Therefore, in saying that the songs are offensive, the Celtic
support can be acted against. Be that as it may, the Bill has
also attacked other supports for the most minor of
misdemeanours, the like of which would normally be
considered par for the course among football fans. This
suggests that the Bill is also an attempt to sanitise football
support across the board.

The 'Green Brigade' is fairly used to offending people with
their political views and expression. That is exactly why
they have been subject to the majority of oppressive
policing. From members being followed home to dawn
raids; arrests with not guilty verdicts to having a camera
thrust in their faces, members of the 'Green Brigade' and
the Celtic faithful have been the victim of frankly heinous
legislation. Alongside the work of FAC something had to
be done.

The first action of note was a self-imposed silence protest in September 2011. Although the Bill wasn't actually passed at that time, it had entered Scottish Parliament and was largely being implemented anyway. In a statement the group said: "Today we held a silent protest against the Offensive Behaviour Bill and the disproportionate policing that we and the wider Celtic support face. It comes on the back of a season when our manager was attacked by bigots because he comes from an Irish Nationalist background. The response of the politicians has been to draft a law that, according to Justice Committee Chair, Christine Graham, is designed to target the Celtic support for our Irish identity and for singing songs in support of Irish nationhood. It looks like the bigots have won." (It continued further).

For the first time since inception, the group sat down in complete silence and unveiled nine banners outlining the proposed laws. Each time a new banner emerged it was applauded and mocked. Some of the laws presented were crazy things like 'No aggressive flag waving', 'No swearing' and 'No lateral movement'. Added to those were materials reading 'Police State' and 'Our songs are not sectarian. Our songs are not illegal. We will not be criminalised. We will not be silenced.' A whistle blew with a quarter of the game to go, which signified the end of speechlessness and a burst into a heartfelt rendition of 'Let the People Sing'. The full stadium joined in with every song and generated a terrific atmosphere. The occasion also saw the first examples of cross stadium chanting - 'C'mon You Boys In Green' and 'Paddy McCourt's Fenian Army'.

Protest banner

Little over a year after the protest, the group were still campaigning against the Bill. In a statement, a Green Brigade spokesman said: "Last Wednesday was a special night at Celtic Park. The display before the match was beyond our wildest expectations, the atmosphere was electric from start to finish and more importantly, Celtic beat arguably the best team in world football. It is a night that will live long in the memory of everyone connected to the Club. However, while the rest of the support were still on Cloud nine, our group was brought back down to earth with a bump as it transpired that Strathclyde Police had visited yet another two members' homes with a view to charging them. To put this into perspective, this means that just under 50% of the Green Brigade have either faced, or are facing a police charge/ban from football." After revealing that shocking statistic, the statement continued: "It has come to the stage where we have to act and fight back. We can't continue to let the Police have free reign to arrest and charge whoever they please. It is having an astronomical effect on people's livelihoods. Those members who are left without a charge can't even enjoy the football anymore in case it leads to a chap at the door that could change their lives forever. The grim reality is that if we don't act now, there may not be a group left come the end of the season. As a result, we have no choice but to highlight this further in the form of a two-match boycott from Celtic Park. This will begin immediately and means that during the forthcoming league match V Inverness Caledonian Thistle and Scottish Cup match V Arbroath, the Green Brigade will not be present whatsoever. Our members live for going to watch and support the team we love, just like every other fan out there. Sadly, we aren't being treated like every other fan and in fact face victimisation and harassment on a scale that is unimaginable. We hope that this boycott will raise awareness of our situation and the end result will be that Strathclyde Police will relent."

The boycott was supported by all season book holders in section 111 both in and out with the group. The matches saw possibly the two worst atmospheres of the season. Still the situation did not improve. After becoming sick of being filmed throughout every match, some members of the Green Brigade spontaneously decided to return the favour and flash their phone cameras back at the police. More joined in. Amazingly the full stadium was awash with flashing camera lights and a chant of "All Celtic Fans against the Bill!" It looked great and highlighted the problem in an inventive and uncontroversial way.

In contempt of the creative efforts, section 111 was closed in August 2013. The Club cited safety issues on the grounds of things such as lateral movement, ceasing to be refrained from. In fairness, their hands were likely tied by Glasgow City Council. Celtic's statement claimed that "If assurances can be made over safety then we may look at this situation again." The Club stayed true to their word. After positive dialogue with the group, section 111 was officially handed back to the 'Green Brigade' by the 23rd of the same month. But with little having improved by way of incrimination, it was inevitable that something would have to give.

Having publicised their ongoing plight, the 'Green Brigade' decided to hold their own protest march in March 2013.

Joined by a healthy number of supporters, marchers gathered at Chrystal Bells pub and then headed further up the Gallowgate in a peaceful manner en route to Celtic Park. Suddenly things turned ugly! Around two hundred police officers were deployed to the scene and instructed to prevent the walk from taking place. The march had not been applied for so it was technically illegal. Instead of acting with humanity, the conduct of the police was absolutely sickening. Peaceful protesters were 'kettled' under a bridge. The crowd was riled but behaved admirably, just chanting "Supporting Your Team Is Not a Crime" and "All Celtic Fans against the Bill." Amid intense intimidation, people began to stray from the area. Yet it was then that the scenes worsened. I urge readers to enter a search for 'Green Brigade peace march attacked' into YouTube, in order to believe the unbelievable, which I am about to recount. Supporters as young as fifteen, walking away from the crowd, were slammed to the ground and handcuffed. Men and women were struck with batons and most haunting of all, a little girl stood crying, terrified as she looked to her horror at the mayhem that Strathclyde Police had created. A lot of supporters caught the violence on camera, many of whom had their phones taken and smashed in an attempt to hide the police's shame. Much survived though and allowed for international media outcry. Dozens of people had been arrested, many more beaten and attacked; all for the crime of walking peacefully in a non-applied march to protest oppressive policing. How ironic that the police conduct showed the actions of a force guilty of exactly that.

The campaign went from strength to strength. A month later FAC held a Demo at George Square, which drew huge numbers. Jeanette Findlay, Joe O'Rourke and a strong presence from the 'Green Brigade', gave voice to the voiceless. In less than phlegmatic fashion, the crowd was told that there would be no more criminalisation of the Celtic support.

The group had achieved the unanimous sympathy of the Celtic faithful. But yet again they went from a position of strength to one of desperation. During a Friday Night Football concept at Fir Park, the 'Green Brigade' disastrously outdid themselves. The group had taken the opportunity to organise a section in their name for the away game at Motherwell. The behaviour in the section cannot be condoned. £10,000 worth of damage was caused by vandalism to seats. The actions of those guilty tarnished the reputation of the 'Green Brigade' to such an extent that it was left in tatters. For Celtic Football Club, it was a matter of a totting up procedure and unfortunately a few bad eggs appeared to have spoilt one of the great revelations of the support. Misery was compounded when Celtic suspended one hundred and twenty eight people seen to be involved with the section and ordered the relocation of a further two hundred and fifty people from 111 to other parts of the ground.

Return:
On one hand, not being at Celtic Park was tough. On the other, it was a chance to reflect on things and re-evaluate the direction of the group. Taking that positivity forward and sticking to their slogan 'Until the Last Rebel', the majority of members elected to take a refund and give up their season books for a time. Through this period, the group's relationship with the Club had all but decimated. However, a conclusion of investigations found suspended members innocent, meaning that there was potential for genuine progress. The group kept their cards very much close to their chest. Their absence was becoming better documented as Celtic Park faded into a morgue like atmosphere. Cleverley, the group allowed the yearnings for them to build and stew. As forums clustered and match day moans mounted – a surprise was in store.
A below average sized crowd clicked through the Parkhead turnstiles and trudged to their seats. BOOM! BOOM! The

unmistakable crash of drumstick and drum pounding together sounded from the distance. The noise pulled closer, sucking attention with it. Eyes were gazing at section 118, situated just next to the away supporters. Then they appeared in all their magnificence. A group of supporters roaring 'The Celtic Song', but who were they? Casual. Satirical. Impactful. Suspicions were confirmed when the 'Green Brigade Ultras' banner was set up at the North West juncture of the stadium. The group sang for ninety minutes and brought a real taste of what had been missing. The players seemed inspired and Celtic turned on the style. Anthony Stokes whipped three past St Johnstone without reply. Speaking post-match, Neil Lennon commented: "I can't thank them (Green Brigade) enough because they made a hell of a difference to the atmosphere today. The players would have thrived on it. I got word this week that they might be in and I was delighted to hear that noise. You tell even just by the rhythm of the game that they added to it." Meanwhile a spokesperson for Celtic Football Club confirmed: "They (Green Brigade) were not banned and they bought individual match tickets."

The spiritual home of the 'Green Brigade Ultras' had always been in section 111 so the group only surfaced irregularly on the terraces. The positive effect that they had made on their returns, presented an opening for renewed discussion with the Club.

After a long silence, the Green Brigade announced that pending finalisations, they'd be back in 111 for the Champions League qualifier against Maribor in August 2014. Frustratingly, access to the section was not granted for this crucial match. It was suggested that relations with the Club could be on the brink of collapse again. Certainly, the bold tone of the group statement ventilated a real sense of infuriation.

Finally, Celtic announced the following on September 17th 2014: "Celtic confirms section 111 will reopen. The reopening follows a period of positive discussions with former Season Ticket holders within the section, during which it has been agreed that the safety of spectators must always be of paramount importance and that the reputation of the Club and its supporters must be protected at all times."

The 'Green Brigade' returned to their rightful place for Motherwell's visit to Celtic Park on September 21st 2014. The match was drawn one each. A refreshing new relationship has been formed between the Club and the group. It looks set to continue.

Celtic Graves Society:
Celtic Graves Society is a very important supporter's group in the history of Celtic Football Club. Their objective is to keep the memories of every person ever connected to Celtic alive. Naturally, the organisation consults the deceased's family and then works alongside them to provide a fitting commemoration. It is appropriate that the Society's slogan is a copy from Willie Maley's quote on Johnny Thompson - 'They never die who live in the hearts they leave behind'.

The root of the Society dates to 2010, when it was noted that Willie Maley's grave was in putrid condition. The widespread solicitude led to the direct establishment of Celtic Graves Society. From that day, the group has stuck to their objective and also worked to safeguard the respectability of resting places for all that have served the Club. Conglomerations of events and commemorations have been carried out over the past five years. One of the earliest was the re-enactment of the pilgrimage to the grave of Johnny Thompson, which was carried out by supporters in 1931. The walk marked the 80th anniversary of Thompson's passing. A long slug, spanning many hours, was well attended. It was a fabulous occasion and a terrific effort. A huge amount was learnt and celebrated, which is the norm for the Society's events.

Celtic Graves Society laid tributes - Johnny Thompson's grave

The group showed conspicuous effort in their memorial service abroad, for former Celt, Charlie Shaw - laid to rest in the USA. Spectacularly, the Society has also managed to locate and identify the resting places of the first ever Celtic team that beat Oldco Rangers 5-2. The campaign took them international again, not least when they ventured to a Johnny Madden commemoration in Prague. Madden had been born in Dumbarton but moved to the Czech Republic to spend six fruitful seasons with Slavia Prague FC. The operation took them from Prague to the USA, to honour Charlie Gorevin. Charlie's tribute was held in Holy Cross Cemetery, Brooklyn, where he and his family had emigrated prior to his passing. The different stages of the journey uncovered new history and revealed facts on the players beyond their careers. A particularly exciting story is that of Philip Murray. The search for the defender found that he had emigrated to Pennsylvania and later paid for his nephew, who went on to become a leader of the American trade union movement, to join him. Additionally, the work of the Society uncovered an old program from a match in our 1931 USA tour. Within it, there is accreditation to Murray travelling some five hundred miles to watch Celtic, showing that since playing in our first ever game, he remained a Celt.

Celtic Graves Society has had many touching impacts on the support. Their involvement in the statue for Jock Stein at the entrance to Celtic Park, and restoration of Brother Walfrid's resting place, are probably the most visual confirmations of that fact. Yet in addition, it could be reckoned that their most special accomplishment was to be able to enshrine the memory of our founding fathers in stone.

On 2nd November 2013 at St Peter's Cemetery in Dalbeth, a short distance from Celtic Park; two hundred people gathered in spite of the rain. They had come to attend the Celtic Graves Society ceremony, in order to unveil a Celtic

Cross in memory of the Club's founding fathers. The cross, shaped out of Mourne Mountain granite from Ireland, stands as permanent laudation to the architects of Celtic, in homage to the Club's roots.

Brendan Sweeney opened the ceremony, before Celtic chairman, Ian Bankier, read out a letter he wrote, imagining what he would say to the founding fathers about our great institution. Celtic FC Foundation CEO, Tony Hamilton, highlighted the ongoing work at the Club and by the support, in adhering to the very principles from which we were founded. Next, former Celtic captain, Tom Boyd spoke of his pride to have done what most dream of and don the green and white hoops as a player. Penultimate, the Society's historian, Terry Dick, gave a splendid speech about Celtic's founding and the social background that they were up against. The Archbishop of Glasgow, Philip Tartaglia, rounded off the ceremony in blessing the monument. It was a great occasion with such a turnout that only Celtic Football Club could conjure.

Away from the ceremonies and commemorations, the Society has become a focal point for anybody wanting to know more about Celtic Football Club and its illustrious history. Members have gathered old photos and memorabilia from the early days of the Club. Others serve as great orators and the wealth of knowledge on not just Celtic's history, but connected institutions and affairs, is quite astounding.

In a nutshell, Celtic Graves Society uses many different methods to bring the history of Celtic and individuals involved, to life. They do a remarkable service to Celtic supporters worldwide.

I think it would be fitting to conclude this subdivision with the words of Terry Dick, said during a special commemoration to Brother Walfrid, a few years ago. "Let us be faithful to our team that has brought such success and distinction to those iconic green and white hoops; but also to the undiminished vision and ideals of Brother Walfrid. His concept of being more than a Club, of a team and a support wearing the garments of inclusion, of tolerance, of honourable behaviour, compassion and charity: ensuring that our grand old team, as it stands on threshold of its 125th year may continue to be worthy of and reaffirm Tom Maley's accolade of almost a hundred years ago, that the Celtic are the greatest and the best of all football and athletic institutions." Terry's words were dripping with passion and struck a chord with me.

Thai Tims:
The Thai Tims are a tear jerking story of football, children, Thailand, Scotland, and of course, English language teaching. The tale commences with a young Thai boy named Berni Lennon. He loves to play football with his brother Steven and like his British born father, he supports Celtic. When Berni was old enough to attend school his parents applied locally, but it soon became apparent that Berni's Down syndrome seemed to pose a barrier to the application process. Schools in the area simply did not have enough resources or training to cope with his needs. In time, the situation started to become desperate as the prospect of travelling fifty miles to a school that could accommodate, became a real possibility.

Parallel to the life of Berni, yet essential to the story, are a Mr. Praman and a Mrs. Yuvaret Sarakoses. Both hold Buddhist beliefs and have considerable influence. These two factors combined to drive a charitable desire and the pair got involved with a project at the Triamsuksanayaiam School in the province of Chanthaburi. They heard of Berni's plight and approached the school. The institute accepted him and he was integrated into the education system at last.

Mr. Praman and Mrs. Yuvaret Sarakoses had attempted to get Berni into many other establishments beforehand - without success. So, to thank the school for their receptiveness, the Lennon's decided to volunteer to teach English to pupils at the school. Despite their best intentions, the couple had limited ability and resources in this department. Therefore they improvised and realised that passion is often the source of much achievement. With that in mind, the two decided to teach children the words of songs sung by Celtic fans. The idea actually proved excellent from a tuition point of view. We have such a literate song book and it was effective in educating large classes quickly. Classrooms were swaying to the sound of 'Fields of Athenry' and 'The Celtic Song'. Only then did these wonderful children become known as the 'Thai Tims'.

The school built on the linguistic breakthrough thanks to YouTube. The teachers started to write songs of their own, adapt existing songs and educate the children to such a level where they felt competent in performing anything from 'This Land' to 'Willie Maley'. Unsurprisingly, once videos of these performances were spotted, they sparkled in public consciousness. Donations to 'The Good Child Foundation' were flooding like valleys in monsoon season. 'The Good Child Foundation' is the charity that Mr. Praman and Mrs. Yuvaret Sarakoses had set up and ran their projects through.

As a result of donations, more Down syndrome children were encouraged to join the school. Things then took a great turn when videos of the Thai Tims started getting played on the big screens at Celtic Park. In no time, Celtic FC Foundation endorsed 'The Good Child Foundation' as one of its official charity partners.

Meanwhile, back in Scotland a then eighteen year old 'Bhoy' (Reamonn Gormley) had just left school. In keeping with the frenetic pace of the Thai Tims rise, he had a couple of months available before going to university, which he put to good use in volunteering to help the Thai Tims. He swiftly jetted off to Thailand and became an icon with the students. A typical day started with Reamonn leading the singing and helping to introduce some slightly more technical English education. In the afternoon, he could be found at the baseball pitch or offering his knowledge, acquired as a youth player at Celtic, to the budding footballers at the school. He spent evenings with the Lennon's, who hosted him. Reamonn was also partial to reeling in fish from the local river with the men living in the area.

After three months of fun, laughter and kindness; he bid farewell. He spoke a few words of Thai and vowed to return to see his new friends the following year. It is absolutely sickening that his promise was unable to come true. Back in Scotland, in February 2011, Reamonn was murdered. He was just nineteen years old. He was a handsome lad with a heart of gold. It is not appropriate to go in to detail but in the interests of clarity for what follows, it should be known that Reamonn was stabbed on his way home from the pub, whilst being mugged.

News of such a fine man's death caused immense anger and a palpable desire to stamp this type of crime out. The Celtic family learned of his volunteering in Thailand and supported 'The Good Child Foundation' with renewed generosity. Whilst they also moved to promote and support an anti-knife crime charity in Scotland, which aims to quell the knife carrying culture in parts of the country.

As Reamonn Gormley would have wanted, the shadow cast by his death inspired Celtic to do further good in his name. 'The Good Child Foundation' released a charity single, 'Just Can't Get Enough'. The song raised thousands of pounds and it sought to promote the charity book 'Berni

Bhoy & The Thai Tims'. The song was hearty, upbeat and included a touching adaptation of the lyrics: 'Reamonn, Jinky and Tommy Burns will be smiling down from heaven on all of us…'

Just when you thought things couldn't get any bigger for the Thai Tims, they smashed the boundaries again. A momentous effort by Berni Lennon's parents paid off, when forty two children were given the opportunity to go to Celtic Park. The Thai Tims were put up by the Club and treated like royalty. A wide range of activities were organised for them in Glasgow.

The children's joy was there for all to see when they sang to the Celtic players at Lennoxtown. From there, they sang with Bertie Auld, met Reamonn Gormley's parents and starred in the CSA Rally. Their joy was reciprocated by thousands, as the children performed songs on the pitch before a home match against St Johnstone.

The trip also encompassed a visit to Glasgow's Archbishop and the Lord Provost. Time was then given for a journey to Celtic's spiritual home across the sea in Ireland. At Belfast, they were given a tremendous welcome and, as usual, smiled their way around the Titanic museum. The group were the headline act for a concert at Belfast City Hall. 'Tell me ma' and other Irish ditties were performed for the benefit of the Lord Mayor, Niall O'Donnghaile.

The excursion also allowed the Thai Tims to perform Scottish/Irish medleys and Celtic songs in front of a packed audience at the Concert Hall back over in Glasgow. The enthusiastic dancing and the love of the performers brought tears to glass eyes.

In 2013 the Thai Tims erected a green and white hall – The Reamonn Gormley Hall in memory of their hero. The charity continues to prosper.

Kano Foundation:

The Kano Foundation is another charity that serves children. The charity was incepted in 2010 thanks to David Hayman after he developed an inspiration from Martin 'Kano' Kane, who had spent a year in hospital battling Devic's Syndrome. The difficulties posed by the neurological condition led to 'Celtic Quick News' running a fundraising campaign: 'Bring Martin Home'. The target was to get Martin back to his family in Perth (Australia) for Christmas. To return home, Martin needed a lot of refurbishment done to the house. A host of fundraising activities including a bucket collection at Celtic Park took place. In the spirit of the Club, the required monetary sum was well exceeded. The left over money, from the £66,000 raised, was spent by taking the children that had volunteered in the bucket collection to Celtic Park for another match. The joy and success of the event paved the way for more. It was then that the Kano Foundation effectively started.

In the words of the charity, their mission is "To treat youngsters, regardless of background and circumstance, to a day out at Celtic Park. Since season 2010/2011 we have given a modern day 'lift over the turnstile' to children varying from boys and girls football teams to local youth clubs and young people with special needs."

Eventually the Kano Foundation gained full support of the Club and is endorsed by being entitled to a section of seating at each match. Thanks to this, they can now accommodate up to seventy two children with thirteen adults, at any one match.

Groups and charities can apply for tickets through the Kano Foundation website. If successful, the children put forward will be greeted by their designated volunteer (ratio of 1 adult per 6 children) and shown to their seats. This will not be done before the kids are handed a goody bag: star studded with refreshments and a Kano Foundation scarf. Volunteers are on hand throughout the match to assist the children with anything that they may need.

After gaining experience, the volunteers found the only issue to be the cost of travel to Celtic Park. This problem has largely been overcome by introducing a 'Supporters Bus Link Up Scheme'. A number of Celtic Supporters Clubs that run buses to matches have officially aligned with them. There are now many routes to the ground covered, offering children very cheap or free bus journeys to and from the stadium.

The Foundation is fully self-funded, relying on the generosity of the Celtic support to donate to their cause. In the last year alone, they have held their annual dinner dance and charity golf days, a skydive, a night showing the Paul Larkin documentary: 'Asterisk Years' and have released an official Kano Foundation song. Hundreds of thousands of pounds have been added to the pot as a result.

The influence of the Foundation has now grown to such a point that the three thousandth child clicked through the turnstyle just before Christmas 2014. Not long after that landmark achievement, the charity patron and inspirer, Martin Kane lost his gallant battle with Devic's Syndrome. David Hayman and the other trustees continue to ensure that the Foundation prospers in his memory - 'Keeping Football Free for Kids'.

"Celtic are blessed having a following that simply defy the elements, whose enthusiasm for the Club is never lukewarm."
Scottish Referee magazine (7 September 1891)

"Celtic FC is the fans, without them there is no club."
Paul McStay

"Celtic enjoys a greater community spirit than any other club in the world."
Archie MacPherson

"Celtic, like Barcelona, are more than a football club. Our clubs are a symbol of a culture and community that has not always been made welcome in their respective countries."
Xavi

"Every professional footballer should seek to play at least one game at Celtic Park. I have never felt anything like it."
Paolo Maldini

"Celtic Park remains the greatest atmosphere that I have ever played in. Their fans are the are the loudest in the world."
Michael Owen

"Celtic fans confirm what I've always known. They are the Greatest. Good luck to Stan and the 60,000 sell-out crowd for today's charity game."
Bernie Slaven

"Celtic fans deserve to be in Europe. The way they were in Barcelona after they had just lost in the way they did was amazing. I have never seen anything like that before."
Messi

"More than a Club, a People."
French Newspaper L'Equipe

Printed in Great Britain
by Amazon